This book belongs to

BETH SMITH

*a woman who desires
to reflect the heart
of Jesus*

May you desire to reflect
the heart of Jesus
everyday.
Love
Fidelia

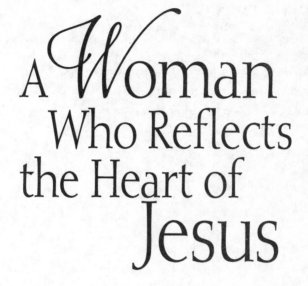

A Woman Who Reflects the Heart of Jesus

Elizabeth George

HARVEST HOUSE PUBLISHERS

EUGENE, OREGON

Cover by Dugan Design Group, Bloomington, Minnesota

Cover photo © Shaun Egan / The Image Bank / Getty Images

A WOMAN WHO REFLECTS THE HEART OF JESUS
Copyright © 2010 by Elizabeth George
Published by Harvest House Publishers
Eugene, Oregon 97402
www.harvesthousepublishers.com

Library of Congress Cataloging-in-Publication Data
George, Elizabeth, 1944-
A woman who reflects the heart of Jesus / Elizabeth George.
    p. cm.
ISBN 978-0-7369-1299-0 (pbk.)
    1. Christian women—Religious life. 2. Devotional literature. 3. Jesus Christ—Example. I. Title.
BV4527.G4645 2010
242'.643—dc22

2010025555

Printed in the United States of America

10 11 12 13 14 15 16 17 18 / BP-SK / 10 9 8 7 6 5 4 3 2 1

Contents

Beginning Your Journey

When you hear the name *Jesus*, what's your first thought? Mine is always the word *perfect*. Jesus is the man who lived a perfect life, had perfect conduct, was perfect in regard to sin, and yet was perfect humanity. But then my thoughts graduate to thinking of this perfect man as the perfect model, the perfect example, the possessor of perfect character, and the perfect person to follow in my quest for spiritual maturity. And that gives me hope.

I've had a terrific time spending months and months poring over hundreds of scriptures and sifting through numerous books on the life of Christ. Can you imagine? It was an outstanding blessing...and a convicting challenge. In the course of my studies I ran across this beautiful and reverent summary of Jesus' life—a summary filled with encouragement for you and me as women who love Him, pray to live like Him, and desire to reflect Him.

> Jesus Christ is everywhere in the New Testament assumed to be the moral and spiritual ideal of the Christian. In His purity of life, perfect obedience to the Father, composure in the hour of persecution, steadfastness in suffering, and resistance to sin, He is the model for the Christian when he enters into similar situations. In this life, we strive to be like the Savior; in our end-time glorification, our souls shall be perfectly conformed to His image.[1]

And now for your trip into 30 incredible character qualities our Savior displayed! As with any journey, you have a destination—Christlikeness. And you get to set your own pace for your travels. You can enjoy one quality a day, or one a week, or find a rhythm that fits your lifestyle. It's just a book, and I want you to read it and enjoy it as a book. But I've also written *A Woman Who Reflects the Heart of Jesus Growth and Study Guide* to help you dig a little deeper into the scriptures that define Jesus' virtues and lead you to personal application. Maybe you and a friend or a small group can go through the study together. (Imagine...unleashing countless women who reflect Jesus into today's world. It will never be the same...and neither will you!)

To fully complete your personal journey to Christlikeness will take a lifetime. You will reach your destination when you cross the threshold of heaven and meet Jesus face-to-face. As you begin, it is my prayer that these 30 scenic viewpoints along the path will help speed you on your way to becoming more like the Master, to becoming *A Woman Who Reflects the Heart of Jesus.*

In His everlasting love,

Elizabeth George

Before You Start: What to Remember About Jesus

You and I have so much to be thankful for because we have the Bible. In it Jesus teaches us what perfect humanity is, and then lives it for us. Jesus is not some celestial, untouchable superstar. He's a person who has lived where we live, faced what we face, and felt what we feel. That's why we can look to Him as a model of Christian behavior. The biblical standards that seem so hard for us to attain are clearly seen in Him. Because He shows us the way as a fellow human, we can follow in His footsteps and live out the same qualities He possessed.

As you embark on this journey through 30 character qualities drawn from Jesus' life, you will only begin to scratch the surface of this most unusual and incredible of all personalities.

As the final verse of the Gospels explains,

> There are many other things that Jesus did, which if they were written one by one, I suppose that even the world itself could not contain the books that would be written (John 21:25).

To say that Jesus was an incomparable person is an understatement! That's why you won't read very far before you discover that many of the scriptural scenarios of Jesus contain multiple lessons and illustrate multiple character qualities. Sprinkled throughout this book you will see some events retold here and there from a different perspective to describe different qualities in Jesus. You will find yourself looking at the same diamond but from another angle.

To help you understand how a man could perfectly model Godlike behavior, and how God could walk among us as an example to follow, here are some important truths to remember about Jesus:

— Jesus was the only man who possessed two distinct natures. His was a personality that, in addition to possessing all the characteristics of the divine nature, had all the qualities of the perfect, sinless human nature as well.

— Jesus did not give up His divine nature. He simply added His human nature. The result of this union was that Jesus accepted certain limitations upon the use of His divine nature (Philippians 2:6-7).

— Jesus did not function independently of either His divine or human natures.

— Jesus' humanity was not the humanity of fallen man, but the humanity possessed by Adam and Eve before their fall.

— Jesus experienced all that we experience as humans, including hunger, thirst, weariness, love, sadness, and even anger, yet without sin.

It is my prayer that each day, as you view another facet of Jesus' lovely life, you will grasp how very special Jesus is as your Lord and Savior, and as a model for how to live as a woman who reflects Him.

Approachable

*W*e live in a marvelous time in history. You can pick up a phone and call anywhere in the world. You can go on your computer, "surf the Net," and order anything from toys to TVs and have them sent to your doorstep. But don't try to talk to a person in this techno-crazy world.

For months—almost a year—my husband Jim has tried to talk to someone, anyone(!), about a phone billing problem and all he ever gets is yet another menu of options. But thankfully, God isn't like that. I can talk to God 24/7, any day of the week at any time! I open my heart and mind and instantly, as always, I'm in His presence. Do you have a problem, a concern, or a request? No worries! Just follow this divine instruction and rest in its assurance: "Let us therefore come boldly to the throne of grace, that we may obtain mercy and find grace to help in time of need" (Hebrews 4:16).

Isn't it comforting to know that God is so utterly approachable? And as we begin our daily walk toward more Christlike character, we see Jesus, God in flesh, modeling this approachability.

Jesus Shows Us the Way

I'm sure you've been near people who, because of their commanding presence, don't seem approachable. Their countenance appears to ooze with superiority. It feels as if it would be the greatest of impositions for you to approach them for anything. Now let me quickly add that this is only your perception. They may be the sweetest, nicest, kindest people on the face of the earth, but something about them makes you hesitant to go up to them.

Well, be thankful this isn't the aura Jesus projected as He, the God of all creation, walked among His creation. Notice how He treated a variety of misfits:

Approachable to the Outcast

Leprosy has historically been a dreadful and frightening disease because its progression is slow, painful, and visible for all to see. Not many years ago, people in Hawaii were so leary of leprosy that they sent all lepers to the island of Molokai.

In Jesus' day, lepers were also feared and considered ceremonially unclean according to Jewish law. They were outcasts from society. A leper was to yell out "Unclean, unclean!" whenever anyone approached or passed nearby. But amazingly, when a leper approached Jesus, He "stretched out His hand and touched him" (Mark 1:41)! The result? The leprosy was immediately cured (verse 42).

To develop Christlike approachability, learn and live these words spoken from the lips and heart of our dear Jesus. He invited any and all, especially outcasts, to "come to Me, all you who labor and are heavy laden, and I will give you rest" (Matthew 11:28).

Reflecting On Your Heart

Your Savior didn't allow the dictates of His society to keep Him from projecting an image that He was approachable. Has your social circle or society dictated how you should treat others, especially those who could be characterized as outcasts? You've been abundantly blessed by God in so many ways. So make it a goal to not look down on those who haven't been so blessed with position, money, clothes, education, or health. Check your heart. Are outcasts able to approach you?

Approachable to the Hopeless

I'm sure you know how it feels to make excellent progress on getting all your work done...only to have the phone ring or someone stop by with an urgent need or a heavy burden. You're a nice person, really! And you enjoy helping others. But when it seems as though someone's need comes at the wrong time (at least according to your plan), you struggle with what to do. You may even find yourself thinking, *Can't you see I'm busy?*

What we need at such a time is a fresh dose of Jesus! He never seemed to allow what was urgent to get in the way of what was important. On one occasion, Jesus was preaching to a packed house, literally (Mark 2:1-5). Not one additional person could fit into the house. As the four friends of a paralytic sought to bring their destitute friend to Jesus for help, the crowded house seemed like a hopeless situation. Yet these friends were convinced that Jesus and only Jesus could help their hopeless friend. Aggressively and persistently, these four men took the tiles off the roof of the house where Jesus was teaching and let their friend's bed down through the hole they had created. Imagine the nerve! And imagine the faith!

At this point Jesus could easily have exclaimed, "What's this man doing here? Can't you see I'm busy? I'm doing urgent work. I'm preaching about God!" But instead, He "saw their faith, [and] He said to the paralytic, 'Son, your sins are forgiven you'" (verse 5). Then Jesus miraculously healed the man's paralysis. Ministering to this one man was what was important, even though the preaching was urgent.

It's the same way when a woman approaches you with some request. Obviously she thinks you can help, and maybe you can. However there's just one problem—you are busy, as always, doing something you determined was important. What to do? This would be a good time to ask yourself, "How would Jesus deal with this lady?"

Reflecting On Your Heart

From the story of the paralytic and his friends, who made sure he had an opportunity to meet with Jesus, and from numerous other instances in the Gospels,

Jesus teaches His followers to be careful not to allow crowds, packed schedules, and busyness to get in the way of people who truly need help. They are what's important. You'll always have something that needs immediate, urgent attention. That's life! But ask God to give you discernment so you don't ignore sincere cries for help. Ask Him, "How would You want me to treat this person?"

Approachable to the Concerned

As a bookend to busyness, there is the idea of being inconvenienced that often becomes an excuse for not appearing to be approachable. You have people to see, places to go, and things to do galore! (There's your busyness!) So in all your spinning about, distraction, and self-focus, you can completely miss the concerns of others. Your rushing, intensity, and appearance give the impression that you might be put out if people approached you.

Not so with Jesus. He had every right to refuse to help a high-ranking Roman military officer who approached Him with a concern for one of his servants, who was suffering. How did Jesus respond? He said, "I will come and heal him" (Matthew 8:7). The Roman centurion, however, who commanded a hundred soldiers, humbly replied, "Lord, I am not worthy that You should come under my roof. But only speak a word, and my servant will be healed" (verse 8). The centurion didn't even ask that Jesus come to his house. The centurion knew this would be a great imposition, so in faith, he asked only that Jesus speak the word, believing in his heart that his servant would be healed when the Lord spoke.

My point is that Jesus was not upset by the man's request. Even though He had just preached possibly the greatest sermon of all time—the Sermon on the Mount—and was being followed by a massive crowd, amazingly, Jesus paid attention to one man's concern (a dreaded Roman at that!). And He had no problem with actually entering the centurion's house to tend to the man's servant. He was willing to suffer the inconvenience of the trip, to turn His back on the business of the moment, to leave the crowds, to take the risk of disapproval, and to suffer the trouble of explaining Himself to the religious leaders who also followed Him, ever looking for reasons to discredit and condemn Him. And yet Jesus was totally approachable.

Reflecting On Your Heart

Anything and everything can be seen as an inconvenience if you want it to be. You can justify and rationalize all day long about why you don't have time for people. There will always be reasons, and some of them good ones, why others shouldn't ask for your time and assistance. But be careful not to put up barriers between you and those you might be able to help. Be flexible. Who knows? Maybe your Plan A might become God's better Plan B as you help someone with a need. To become more like Jesus, purpose and pray to be approachable like He was...and still is to you today and every day.

Approachable to the Unimportant

Who is the most important man who ever lived? Without a doubt it's Jesus Christ! As such, Jesus could also have been the most isolated, insulated, protected person who ever lived, right? But amazingly, He was just the opposite. As we're learning, Jesus could be approached by anyone, and it appears also at any time.

A scene in Matthew 19 proves this all too well. Here, "little children were brought to Him that He might put His hands on them and pray" (verse 13). Obviously the parents of these little ones perceived Jesus was approachable. However, the well-meaning disciples thought Jesus was too important to be bothered with and by children and tried to send the parents and their young ones away. What was Jesus' response? "'Let the little children come to Me, and do not forbid them; for of such is the kingdom of heaven.' And He laid His hands on them" (verses 14-15).

As a Christian, you are important! You are important to God, and you're important to your family and friends. But sometimes, in a prideful moment, it's easy to forget that you cannot use your knowledge, accomplishments, and position to justify being unapproachable to others, no matter how important your achievements may seem. Like those little children, all people are important to God and merit our love, attention, and ministry if and when it is needed.

I work hard on appearing approachable. Sometimes when I'm at church or speaking at a conference, I sense women hesitating or thinking twice about speaking to me. Some even turn away in uncertainty. But my ministry is to women, and I truly do want to visit and talk and listen and help. In fact, that's my heart and my joy.

So I've learned to do a few things to appear more accessible to others. First, I have a personal motto wherever I go—"Go to give." This is my time with the women, with people. I've come down out of my writing perch to go *out!* And my outing has been prayed over and eagerly anticipated and may be my one and only opportunity to visit with a particular group of women. Once I get there, I smile—a lot! Then I try to touch as many of God's sheep as I can. I take the initiative and speak to, encourage, and even affirmatively touch as many women as I can. I don't know if Jesus smiled, but I do know He was a cheerful giver and He was approachable. No one was unimportant to Him. Oh, to be like Him!

Approachable to the Outsiders

Racism is not a new concept. Nor is male chauvinism a brand new behavior. Both were in vogue during the time of Jesus. The Jews were especially prone to believe that because they were God's chosen people, they were better than everyone else. Therefore they had nothing to do with the rest of humanity, the Gentiles! Women were also held in low regard at this time. But amazingly one Gentile (non-Jewish) woman perceived that Jesus was approachable, fell at His feet, and asked Him to cast a demon out of her daughter (Mark 7:24-30).

As you read through this encounter in the Bible, you might initially think Jesus was being unkind and demeaning as He addressed this suffering woman. But the fact that He, a teacher, would even speak to a foreign woman was a big deal! As He tested her faith, saying His first responsibility was to the Jews as promised by God,

He was also making allowances for Gentiles, including this woman. No other leader in all of Israel would have even had this conversation with her, let alone tell her to "go your way; the demon has gone out of your daughter" (verse 29). What a bright example of the effect of being approachable!

Just because someone seems "different" to you doesn't justify an avoidance mentality. Jesus put Himself in a place where a foreigner *and* a woman—an outcast on two counts—could approach Him. God never intended for the Jews to isolate themselves from the rest of the world. And God's intentions haven't changed for you and me today. We are to go into the world and rub shoulders with different ethnic groups. We are not to avoid them but emulate Jesus, accept their differences, and be ready when they approach us in their hour of need.

Approachable to the Insincere

I've been emphasizing the importance of being approachable. Normally for most women this is not a problem. In general, women are there for others, especially their family and friends. When someone needs us, we're ready to help. But how do you handle a person who says she wants your advice or assistance, yet once you've given it, she disregards it or does the opposite?

This definitely happened to Jesus! Often He was approached by people who said they wanted help, but deep down they didn't. For instance, Mark 10:17-22 gives us a perfect example of such a person, who approached Jesus to ask, "Good Teacher, what shall I do that I may inherit eternal life?" (verse 17).

This is probably the most important question anyone can ever ask. Yet Jesus knew this young man's heart and knew how fond he was of his money. So Jesus gave him a test to see what he was willing to give up. Jesus told this rich young ruler to "sell whatever you have and give to the poor, and you will have treasure in heaven; and come, take up the cross, and follow Me" (verse 21).

Jesus loved this young man (verse 21), wanted to help, and was willing to. But basically the man didn't want Jesus' help. He seemed to say and do all the right things, yet ultimately he left Jesus because he was unwilling to obey and follow Jesus.

Sadly, you will have encounters like this. You're approachable, people know it, and some will seek your assistance. But they will not sincerely want to follow your advice and will reject your help. These are sad and sometimes hurtful experiences. Your initial response may be to withdraw and wall yourself off from being hurt again by others.

Please don't succumb to these kinds of thoughts. God has gifted and prepared you with the help you can give to so many others who are sincere and desperately need what you have to offer! Try to forget those who used and abused you. Get up and dust yourself off. Then pray for them and ask God to again give you a heart that seeks to follow Jesus and be approachable. After all, one of the 12 disciples betrayed Jesus and yet Jesus still gave His life and blood as a ransom for those who approach the cross.

Reflecting the Heart of Jesus

Being approachable is a subtle quality. You may think, *Of course anyone could talk to me or ask something of me!* But you may also be conveying just the opposite attitude. Think again about Jesus' approachability. Are you sure you are approachable? To your husband and children? To the people at church, at work, or next door? Is your heart tuned in to those who are outcasts, hopeless, concerned and needy, seemingly unimportant outsiders, even the insincere?

Jesus meant it when He said, "Come to Me, all you who labor and are heavy laden, and I will give you rest" (Matthew 11:28). Ask God for His love. Pray for an approachable spirit that will reflect the heart of Jesus, the One who never refused the cries of anyone who was in need and sincerely seeking help...including you!

~ A Prayer to Pray ~

Lord Jesus, thank You that You have always been approachable in my times of need. May I reflect Your heart and be ready to receive others who need Your help through me. Amen.

Available

My husband Jim has taught me volumes about what it means to be available. As a pastor and seminary professor, wherever his office was, there was a line outside his door. I used to tease him that he needed a Take-a-Number machine! No matter how busy he was (and believe me, he was so busy there seemed to be a dust cloud behind him!), Jim was somehow always available to those he led, worked with, introduced to Christ, mentored, and taught. As his wife, I had to learn to expect to do some serious waiting and hanging around anytime we went to church because he was available. Even after his students graduated or people moved away, many of them still call or e-mail Jim. And you guessed it—he is still available.

Also, when I think of the women who have cared about me and poured their knowledge of Christ into my life, I have to thank God for how available they were to me. I know they were super-busy, and yet they made time—to meet with me, to pray with me and for me, to give advice when needed, and always to provide an abundance of encouragement. I'll probably never know the sacrifices they made to spend time with me. I owe them a huge debt for their part in helping me to grow in Christ…and hopefully to take on some small resemblance to His magnificent character.

Jesus Shows Us the Way

Perhaps you already have a mentor in your life as you continue to grow as a Christian. Whether you do or not, you still have the ultimate mentor and example in Jesus. No one is more available than He is. He is ever-present. With a simple prayer like Peter's three-word cry for help—"Lord, help me!"—when he was sinking into the Sea of Galilee, you can reach Jesus in a nanosecond. As the Bible says, "The eyes of the Lord are on the righteous, and His ears are open to their prayers" (1 Peter 3:12).

Have you ever thought about what it cost Jesus to become available to mankind? To begin, at some point in eternity past, before there was time, Jesus willingly accepted the Father's plan for Him to take on a human body so He could dwell among us. He also humbled Himself to become human so He could serve as the perfect sacrifice for sin. Jesus volunteered for the task of coming to earth to save and minister to those He created. He made Himself available to the Father before time. And that availability continued during Jesus' earthly ministry.

Today we are exposed to yet another rich character quality Jesus possessed, that of availability. As is the case with all of the qualities spotlighted in this book, availability was perfectly lived out in Jesus. That means we can learn about availability, see it in His lovely life, and by His grace, imitate it. As we begin looking at this important virtue, you might wonder how this quality differs from that of approachability. I'm glad you asked!

Approachability has the idea of a passive, friendly attitude. It involves how others perceive you from a distance. Being approachable means that someone could look at you or me and sense that we're friendly and easy to talk to. They might even notice that others are able to reach out to you and not get put off or dismissed or snubbed. Do you recall how Jesus modeled this quality in the previous chapter? Do you remember how the foreign woman felt she could come to Jesus with a request for her ailing daughter? And how the parents of the little children—and even the children themselves—had no hesitancy about coming to Jesus and gathering around Him? Even someone like the rich young ruler—someone Jesus knew wouldn't do what He said and wouldn't follow Him—felt like he could approach the Lord and ask Him questions and talk with Him.

Availability has a more active posture. It often takes the initiative to reach out. The available person is a ready person, prepared and eager to respond when she believes she can help and has something to give. My mind just flashed to the prophetess and judge Deborah. This woman sat under a palm tree and waited for the children of Israel to come to her for help and judgment (Judges 4:4-5). Then when Barak, a military leader of Israel, requested her presence during a vital battle, she gladly went with him (Judges 4:4-9). And now my thoughts are rushing to Elizabeth, who was available and opened her home and heart to the newly pregnant Mary, the soon-to-be mother of our Lord.

But I want us to focus on Jesus. Doesn't the term *available* describe Him? We'll soon see that He was just such a person—the Perfect Person, always ready and available to respond because He knew He could help. In fact, that was part of His life mission: "The Son of Man did not come to be served, but to serve, and to give His life a ransom for many" (Matthew 20:28). Let's watch Him now as He walked on earth, totally available.

Give Me a Drink

Jesus had barely begun His ministry when He came from Jerusalem to Samaria on His way to Galilee. The shortest route was through Samaria, an area filled with a mixed race of people the Jews despised. Even though Jesus was the Word become flesh (John 1:14), He still felt the effects of the physical limitations of His human body. He and His disciples had been walking since early morning. It was high noon when His group stopped in Samaria at a well for a drink of water (John 4:6). There Jesus sat down at the town well while the disciples went into the local village for food. While they were gone, a lone woman approached the well to draw water. It was unusual for a woman to come to the well alone. And it was also an odd time of day for her to do so, because women usually approached the well early or late in the day to avoid the heat. This woman—generally referred to as "the woman at the well"—also had a bad reputation (see verses 16-18).

As the woman approached the well, Jesus took the initiative and spoke to her, asking her to "give Me a drink" (verse 7). Jesus broke all social, religious, and racial customs by opening a conversation with this woman.

Jesus sensed this woman had a need, and He knew He could help. You can read their full conversation in verses 7-26. In the end, not only did this woman respond to Jesus' offer of spiritual help, but so did the entire village! That's quite a response—and it was all because Jesus was willing to break a few social rules and be available.

=== *Reflecting On Your Heart* ===

> The gospel is for every person. It was meant to be shared to the ends of the earth with any and all, regardless of race, social position, religious background, or past or present moral state. Do you think your heart is broken for those who are lost? And are you prepared, willing, and available to share "the good news" of Jesus Christ at any time and in any place and to any one? Even if this challenge makes you a little uncomfortable, at least you can make yourself available by reaching out with kindness and concern. Like Jesus, just genuinely care and be available.

Everyone Is Looking for You

Do you ever feel by the end of most days that everyone is looking for you? Maybe you even feel like this when your day is just beginning! Your husband, children, boss, parents, women's committee, and prayer chain at church are all clamoring for a piece of you. Well, in a small way, you are getting an idea of how Jesus may have felt on one particular day that is described in Mark 1:29-39. Here's how His day went after teaching in the synagogue and dealing with demons. Notice that however physically tired or drained He already was, His heart was with the people and He was available to keep right on reaching out to them, one after another.

～ He reached out and healed Peter's mother-in-law in the house (verse 31).

⁓ He reached out and healed all who were waiting outside the house (verse 32).

⁓ He reached out to the rest of the city as word spread that He was available to help them (verses 33-34).

⁓ He reached out to all Galilee after being directed through prayer to be available to those in other towns in the area (verses 35-39).

As you know all too well, being available is demanding. You can quickly become exhausted by the incessant demands on your time and energy. So how do you decide who gets—and truly needs—your attention and care?

Here's one way Jesus answered this question. The day after the one just described, He prepared Himself for another people-packed day by getting up early before everyone else, disappearing to a quiet spot, and praying (verse 35).

The results? Prayer refreshed God's Son for what would be expected of Him during the new day in front of Him. Prayer also gave Him direction for the day. The disciples wanted Him to stay and capitalize on the excitement and success of the previous day's ministry. "When they found Him, they said to Him, 'Everyone is looking for You'" (verse 37). But Jesus, having received the Father's agenda while praying, answered, "Let us go into the next towns, that I may preach there also" (verse 38).

Reflecting On Your Heart

It's right and it's Christlike to be available, but you can't go every place or minister to every need. So make sure you get clear direction for each new day. Start by praying. Like Jesus, check in with the Father for His lead. Then begin at home by being available to your family.

While He Spoke...

Many times, being available becomes the complementary twin

of being approachable. This was definitely the case with Jesus on one occasion. He was deeply involved in a question-and-answer session when, "while He spoke these things to them, behold, a ruler came and worshiped Him, saying, 'My daughter has just died, but come and lay Your hand on her and she will live.' So Jesus arose and followed him, and so did His disciples" (Matthew 9:18-19).

While this band was on the way to the ruler's house, Jesus was interrupted again when a woman who had been sick with bleeding for 12 years reached out and touched the hem of His garment. Jesus was on a mission...but He stopped, turned around, and healed the woman (verses 20-22). Finally, Jesus entered the ruler's house, only to encounter yet another obstacle He needed to deal with: Some professional mourners were already there creating a noisy and chaotic ruckus (verses 23-24). After putting them all out of the house, the Lord was at last able to take the dead girl by the hand and bring her back to life (verses 24-26).

Reflecting On Your Heart

Life and ministry are never simple. That's because people are involved. Maybe if you cloistered yourself in a monastery somewhere, things might be much simpler. But to what end? Who would benefit from such an existence? Jesus definitely showed us a better way as He walked among the people and was clearly open and available to them. Yes, the chaos and pressure do sometimes escalate, but at the end of a day of assisting others, people are helped and miracles happen—not the kinds of miracles Jesus executed, but miracles of hope and assurance, of love and comfort. It all begins with being available. To be blessed—and a blessing— be available.

Your Brother Will Rise Again

Throughout the Gospels three names pop up several times— Lazarus, Martha, and Mary. This trio was made up of a brother and two sisters. They were close to each other, and they were close friends of Jesus. We'll meet Martha and Mary on other occasions in this book, but for now, meet their brother, Lazarus. Unfortunately, Lazarus is dying, and Jesus is asked by his sisters to come and heal him (John 11:1-5).

There was just one problem: The religious leaders had already tried to kill Jesus (verse 8), so returning to Bethany was extremely dangerous. In fact when Jesus decided to go visit Lazarus, His disciple Thomas resignedly stated, "Let us also go, that we may die with Him" (verse 16). The disciples thought they would be killed right along with Jesus. Jesus sovereignly knew that His time to die would not come while He was at Lazarus' house, but this scene shows us that being available may sometimes place us in difficult situations.

Thomas and the other disciples were ready to go with Jesus even though they realized the danger that might await them. Confidence and courage often come down to trusting Jesus and being obedient. Yes, being available is scary. And things do happen! But power and blessings await you on the other side of the first step of faith and obedience—being available. When Jesus arrived at Martha's house, Lazarus was already dead and buried, yet He had promised Martha that "your brother will rise again" (verse 23). Because the disciples were there, they were blessed to witness Christ miraculously raise Lazarus from the dead!

I Must Stay at Your House

Normally it's easy to make yourself available to family, friends, and others who are on your "like list." But what about being available to those on your "dislike list"? Now, that's a different story, isn't it?

Jesus shows us a better way as we look at the tax collector named Zacchaeus. His story is found in Luke 19:1-10. Here we see Jesus moving toward Jerusalem and His impending death. When Zacchaeus heard that Jesus was passing his way, he climbed into a tree to get a better look at Jesus. As Jesus walked by, He noticed Zacchaeus and took the initiative, saying, "Zacchaeus, make haste and come down, for today I must stay at your house" (verse 5).

Even though Zacchaeus was considered a cheater and traitor,

Jesus made Himself available to him. In response to Jesus' friendly advance, Zacchaeus vowed to give back any excessive taxes he had collected, offering even more than was considered to be normal restitution. As Jesus had been available to him, Zacchaeus was now making himself and his money available to others. This was the fruit of his conversion.

Being available was a powerful tool in the hands of Jesus. With only an overture, He conveyed love, respect, a caring heart, and an ability to help. Zacchaeus was a lonely and ostracized man. What he craved was for someone to recognize him and show him some attention. All Jesus had to do was call out his name—*Zacchaeus*.

Take a look around. There are people like Zacchaeus everywhere. They are looking for someone who is available to listen and sympathize with their pain, to give them a kind word. And once you begin to establish relationships, who knows? Those people may even embrace the good news of Jesus Christ as the One who loves them and is ever available to meet their spiritual needs.

Reflecting the Heart of Jesus

We began this chapter looking at Jesus' availability to the Father and His willingness to submit Himself to becoming human—with all its limitations—so He could be available to mankind. This availability was constant all through His brief time of ministry. And it continued as He made Himself available as the perfect sacrifice, to the point of death. And now His availability continues as "He is also able to save to the uttermost those who come to God through Him, since He always lives to make intercession for them" (Hebrews 7:25).

How could you and I not respond to the example Jesus has set before us? Yet, in our selfishness we're tempted to cling to our privacy. We think we need our space. We selfishly hold on to the many benefits and resources Jesus has given us to share with others. And Jesus certainly never intended His people (us included) to hoard their salvation and its resultant blessings.

Instead, our Lord wants us to start up a conversation with others like the woman at the well. He means for us to stretch ourselves each day reaching out to people like He did on possibly His busiest day on planet Earth. And He gives us the grace to be available to the needs of those who are suffering, those like the man whose daughter died, and the woman with the 12-year illness, and the sisters whose brother was dead—even a Zacchaeus type who was curious about Jesus.

Prayer is the perfect place to start! Ask God to open your heart, your eyes, and your ears—maybe even your wallet—to others. Make it a daily goal to be friendly, to smile, to be ready and available to reflect the big heart of Jesus.

⌐ A Prayer to Pray ⌐

O Father, I need Your help! Show me how to balance my busyness with being a better representative of You. May I remember Your complete availability to me when my heart cried out to You. Give me eyes that see, ears that hear, and a heart that responds to the needs of others. Thank You...and amen.

Compassionate

*M*aybe you've been through what I experienced this past week. You know something's wrong. You don't like the way you're behaving or thinking. You can't believe how callously you're treating others or responding to people. You're off-kilter and you know it. You're not your "good self"—the self you want to be and seek to be. And you're certainly in no way acting like a woman who's filled with the Holy Spirit and walking with Jesus.

Feeling all of the above, I sat down earlier today to inventory the past week. I stopped all my busyness and devoted time to looking into my heart. I wanted to see if I could put my finger on what was missing, because I didn't like the way things (and I!) were going. Surprise of surprises, my heart-search took only a few minutes before I came face-to-face with the reality that a major character quality had been missing in me and my heart for the past week or so. It was *compassion*.

I think one reason I had slipped so badly that compassion appeared at the top of my Spiritual Needs List is because it's the beginning of a new year...and I'm already behind. I had such great plans and dreams for myself. For starters, there were things around the house that I meant to fix, finish, clean out, organize, or improve last year. And once the Christmas decorations were all down and put away, I was so ready to dive into these projects for real. The facts? To date (and today is January 8!), zero has been done on this list.

And then there's my stack of thank-you notes I was going to

write right away, before it got embarrassingly late. (Last year I said I'd never do that again!) And yet, there they sit. If I don't take care of this pile soon, I'll have to start dusting it!

And my resolutions and the new disciplines I was going to put into place (at last) this year (even if it kills me)? Zero again!

Just about nothing has happened in over a week in these areas of the poor pathetic life I've eked out so far this brand new year. And what's happened instead? I've been irritable, frustrated, even weepy. And instead of falling upon the Father in prayer, I've turned up my efforts, drive, and determination to even higher levels to help me in my pursuit of progress in these areas. Amazingly, my fleshly efforts to be productive changed my habits and backfired. Gone was any hint of what should be lovely and Christlike in my actions and attitudes.

Jesus Shows Us the Way

When I think of compassion, I always recall a string of words used often in the Gospels that have stuck with me. In fact, I can't shake them, even if I wanted to. They describe our Lord and Savior, Jesus Christ. On a number of occasions in the Bible, Jesus is described as being "moved with compassion." These words are preceded by a scene in which a person is in need. And they are followed by some caring, kind, helpful act from Jesus. It's true that a picture is worth a thousand words, so walk with me now through some instances of compassion that occurred in Jesus' days of ministry on earth.

The Displays of Compassion

SCENE 1

The first photo we want to peer over was snapped in Mark 1:40-42. Jesus was on the move. He had begun His official public ministry. As He healed the sick and cast out demons, His fame spread. So much so that, wherever He went, multitudes showed up, bringing along those they knew who were sick or possessed by evil spirits.

If you think your life is busy and hectic—and challenging—and if you think you're embroiled in a serious ministry to people, you'll want to note that Jesus' days were unbelievably full. After He cast out an evil spirit in Capernaum, the Bible reports that "His fame spread throughout all the region around Galilee" (Mark 1:28). Then, after He stayed with His disciple Peter and healed Peter's mother-in-law, the whole city gathered in front of Peter's door and "brought to Him all who were sick and those who were demon-possessed" (verse 32). Everywhere Jesus went, the people descended upon Him with their needs. Talk about a challenge! And talk about chaos!

In this first photograph, Jesus was approached by a man with leprosy and enough faith in Christ to say, "If You are willing, You can make me clean" (verse 40).

The very next words in the Bible report that "Jesus, moved with compassion, stretched out His hand and touched him" (verse 41). The result of Jesus' compassion—and His power? The poor man was completely cleansed of leprosy. Unlike the people, who rejected and retreated from lepers, Jesus reached out and touched this pitiful leper.

SCENE 2

Another magnificent snapshot of Jesus' compassion is captured in Mark 6:30-32. This time there were no lepers or strangers in need. No, it was Jesus' very own disciples, tired and exhausted from ministry. They weren't complaining, and they didn't ask Jesus for anything. But He sensed their weariness and their lack of solitude, rest, and relaxation. So, because throngs of people were coming and going and gathering in Capernaum, He took the initiative, beckoning them to "come aside by yourselves to a deserted place and rest a while" (verse 31). Sympathizing and empathizing with these faithful-but-tired men, the Savior suggested a time away from ministry for His friends' refreshment and to give them an opportunity to regain their strength.

I love this scene that highlights Christ's tender care for His disciples. He was aware of the toils of His disciples and the toll it had taken on them. In His compassion, He came up with a plan that would provide relief for them from the constancy of ministry—rest for their tiredness, and refuge from the masses, not to mention time in His very presence!

SCENE 3

You can probably guess what happened as soon as the disciples got into a boat with Jesus and sailed to another location to enjoy that much-needed R & R away from the crowds. The masses (about 5000-plus!) in this new place recognized the group, spread the word, and a multitude quickly ran and gathered where they had retreated. In fact, the people got there before the boat carrying Jesus and the disciples arrived. There went the disciples' chance for any privacy and restoration (verses 32-33)!

The response to the masses and their needs? Prepare yourself to witness two—no, make that three!—compassionate responses.

First, we read about Jesus' initial reaction: "And Jesus, when He came out, saw a great multitude and was moved with compassion for them." Why? "Because they were like sheep not having a shepherd." And what did He do about this condition and need? "He began to teach them many things…[until] the day was…far spent" (verses 34-35). Unlike perhaps you and me, Jesus was not upset. He didn't fall apart because His plan was thwarted. He wasn't frustrated or upset with the people. And He wasn't irritated by this interruption. No, He was moved with compassion. The people had no shepherd! So Jesus, the Shepherd, fed the massive flock spiritual food, teaching them about the kingdom of God (Luke 9:11). He also healed those who had need of healing.

Next, we view compassion through the eyes of the disciples. As the hours passed and daylight's end drew closer, the disciples also had compassion for the multitude. We hear their hearts in these words spoken to Jesus: "This is a deserted place, and already the hour is late. Send them away, that they may go into the surrounding country and villages and buy themselves bread, for they have nothing to eat" (Mark 6:35-36).

On the surface, their request may seem harsh. But their concern was genuine and accurate. The people had come many miles to be with Jesus in a remote spot, possibly leaving their homes and towns on the spur of the moment when they heard Jesus had been spotted nearing the shore. They hadn't brought food with them, and darkness was approaching. The disciples' compassionate solution? Dismiss the meeting before it became too dark and send the throng home so they could eat and find a place to spend the night.

And then it was Jesus' turn to once again show compassion. He turned to the disciples who had suggested Plan A, a practical solution to a large problem—"send them away." Ever the perfect planner, Jesus presented Plan B (B meaning Better and Best!)— "You give them something to eat" (verse 37). Of course, that was impossible when you're looking at a group of more than 5000 men (not to mention the women and children who accompanied them)! So Jesus performed the impossible—a miracle. He multiplied five loaves of bread and two fish, supplying enough food for the people to be filled. And amazingly, there were 12 baskets of food left over (verses 37-44)!

The Model of Compassion

Compassion was Jesus' specialty. As I've already mentioned, He was moved with compassion. We know that compassion means taking pity on the condition of others. To be compassionate is to be merciful, to be filled with sympathy and mercy. Compassion cares. In fact, it cares deeply. And it prays, thinks, searches, and seeks to help those in need with what they need. And it does the work required to give the care, even when tired, even late into the night, even all night. It stems from a genuine concern for the sufferings or misfortunes of others.

And no one can match Jesus when it comes to compassion. He, being God in flesh, is the most compassionate man who ever lived and walked the earth. For Him it came naturally, meaning it was His nature, His divine nature. He was perfect, and so was His compassion. And thankfully, we can nurture compassion. We can grow in this heart condition. We can pray and purpose to take a greater interest in others, to feel their hurts and respond with a mixture of pity and help. And, praise God, we can pore over and learn from the photo album of Christ's caring compassion in the living Word of God.

What's left behind in our hearts and actions when something as lovely and Christlike as compassion is missing? I know the answer to this question. What's left behind is something shockingly ugly! Without compassion we live in the opposite realm—a realm of coldheartedness and ruthlessness.

After the inward look—the heart-check—there's the upward

look! When we recognize our sinful ugliness and purpose to stop it, to put it away, and ponder the beauty and loveliness of Jesus and His compassion, we are moved and shamed...yet inspired, instructed, and encouraged by His utter kindness.

Reflecting the Heart of Jesus

Compassion and concern marked the Master's attitude toward those who were poor, unfortunate, and downcast. And Christ also showed concern for those who ministered alongside of Him. We too should have this balanced compassion. For instance, sometimes we're quicker to experience and express compassion for the unfortunate and the helpless than we are for those who are spiritually mature and forging ahead in the Lord's work. We're usually willing to supply food, water, shelter, and money to the poor and needy. But why is it we expect so much of those who are the church superheroes, those who are expected to keep on keeping on, to do the work of the ministry? It's easy to think, *Hey, they've been trained for their service. They've been equipped for the long haul. Aren't they the strongest of the strong? They knew what they were getting into. So what's the big deal if they're tired? We're all tired!*

I know firsthand from my husband's days in the ministry what a blessing little acts of compassion were to our family. Jim gave fully, joyfully, and he expected nothing in return. And this kind of compassion bestowed upon him and our family here and there along the way by sensitive believers were seen as gifts from God!

Do you know any missionaries you can spoil when they come home on furlough? Do you have the finances to give your pastor and his wife a night away in a nice hotel? Is there someone at church who serves unceasingly and could put a dinner-out gift certificate to good use, being refueled and refreshed at the same time?

Who can you reach out to today in compassion? One thing I pray to do daily is be on the lookout for those in need. Nothing as dramatic as a leper, but someone, anyone, in need. Such a prayer reminds me to put on a heart of compassion—to follow in Jesus' footsteps and have compassion for one another.

~ A Prayer to Pray ~

Dear Jesus,
Fill my heart with compassion and care
For those who need help or live in despair.
Break my heart 'til it's able to see
Those who could use some kindness from me.
Amen.

Confident

*Y*ou've probably read or heard about people who are afraid to leave their houses. They have their groceries and other supplies dropped off by delivery people at the front door. They never leave the house, and few are ever allowed to enter. Such people have a serious phobia. A *phobia* is an extreme or irrational fear of something, and it seems like there are as many phobias as there are people who have them. Like most people, you probably have your own area of fear or concern about some aspect of life. It probably doesn't fall into the phobia category, but it's there. Maybe you're nervous about speaking in public, driving your car on the freeway, flying on an airplane, or going to the dentist. Whatever it is, you are less than confident about participating in anything that is connected to that area of concern.

Reading this book might not cure you of your area of concern, but hopefully you will gain some insight into the issue of trust as it relates to a biblical understanding of confidence.

Jesus Shows Us the Way

Today we approach a powerful quality in our Lord's life—confidence. It's a virtue that gave Him boldness and courage to live out God's will for His life. You'll find an incredible resource for managing your challenges as you peer through the lens of Scripture at Jesus' confidence.

As we begin, consider the meaning of confidence. A bottom-line understanding of this quality begins with trust. Confidence suggests a feeling of certainty as one trusts in his or her own abilities. The "self-made" person has a firm trust in their education, professional abilities, athletic skills, looks, health, and material resources. Their belief in themselves produces a state of mind or a manner that is marked by easy coolness and freedom from uncertainty, self-doubt, or embarrassment. As long as they can trust in themselves, they believe they are invincible. In their minds, there's nothing they can't accomplish.

But there's another kind of confidence, and it too is based on trust. However, it's not a trust in self, but a trust in God. Who better to demonstrate the confidence that comes from trusting God than God's only Son, the Lord Jesus? We first observe this character quality boldly lived out in Jesus at an early age.

I Must Be About My Father's Business

The adolescent years are an awkward age for most children. These teens and preteens want to grow up so badly, yet when they're given opportunities to accept adult responsibilities, they usually retreat back to their safety zones. Their desire to be more adultlike is sometimes overridden by their hesitancy to grow into new areas of duty. Their fear of failure can stifle them. But the young Jesus was different.

Even at the age of 12, Jesus' confidence was obvious as Mary, His mother, and Joseph "found Him in the temple, sitting in the midst of the teachers, both listening to them and asking them questions. And all who heard Him were astonished at His understanding and answers" (Luke 2:46-47). Mary and Joseph asked Jesus why He was there in the temple. They had been earnestly looking for Him, thinking He was lost. To them the young Jesus responded, "Why did you seek Me? Did you not know that I must be about My Father's business?" (verse 49).

Jesus was surprised that Mary didn't understand and had forgotten His divine role in the Godhead that had been clearly communicated to her by the angel Gabriel. Even at this early age, Jesus had a keen awareness of His identity. At age 12 He showed bold confidence in His mission. He was already busy preparing for the special work the Father had for Him.

=== *Reflecting On Your Heart* ===

Like the Lord's confidence in His Father, your confidence must come from your identity in and with Jesus. He has made you a new creation (2 Corinthians 5:17) and given you a fresh start. Your past has been forgiven. The slate of your sins has been erased. Your present is empowered by Jesus' Spirit. And your future is guaranteed for all eternity. You are one with Christ. Therefore, there's no reason to be fearful of anything. Oh, you must have a healthy respect for the fragility of life and the need for wisdom and safety precautions. But there's no reason to be anxious about your normal activities. Remember, confidence is based on trust. If your confidence for some challenge is wavering, maybe you've lost sight of who it is you are to trust. Trusting in yourself is shaky ground. Trust instead in the rock that is solid, in Jesus Christ. "Blessed is the man who trusts in the LORD, and whose hope is the LORD" (Jeremiah 17:7).

Do Not Fear

In another scene, Jesus prayed all night and then selected His disciples to follow Him and be trained for future ministry (Matthew 10:16-26). Jesus began to give them instructions before sending them out in twos for ministry. He cautioned them, explaining, "I send you out as sheep in the midst of wolves" (verse 16). He then ran through a list of all sorts of horrible things that might happen to them as they ministered in His name. They would even be accused of working for Satan (verse 25)!

This doesn't seem like a very good way to instill confidence in a newly appointed evangelistic team, does it? A talk like that would be enough to make most people resign and turn in their prophet's badge! But Jesus wanted to give His new team a realistic picture of what they would face. He told them the truth. He prepared them and made them wiser about what was really out there.

But Jesus wasn't finished. On the heels of the negative came the positive. To ensure that the disciples' confidence wouldn't waver, He ended His pep talk with an assurance of God's care. He clearly communicated that the same God who takes care of the insignificant little sparrow would surely take care of them. Jesus then told them, "Do not fear therefore; you are of more value than many sparrows" (Matthew 10:31).

Reflecting On Your Heart

God places great value on you. Savor this truth! In fact, you are so valuable that He sent His only Son to die for you (John 3:16). And because of God's love, you never need to be afraid of personal threats or difficult trials. This should cause you to have a different perspective on your life. Yes, times of trouble will come, but rather than cowering in fear, have the confidence to trust your all-wise and loving heavenly Father. The wolves are out there, but the Good Shepherd knows that you are one of His sheep. He is always there with you and for you. Therefore, "do not fear."

Believe...in Me

In case you haven't noticed the thread, Jesus' disciples were confident only as long as they were in His presence. But when Jesus told them during their last supper that He was leaving, they were shaken to the core. Their confidence fell to an all-time low. That seems to be why Jesus was telling His troubled disciples not to worry: "Let not your heart be troubled; you believe in God, believe also in Me" (John 14:1).

But here's an update: The disciples' confidence returned after Jesus' resurrection and the coming of the Holy Spirit, and they went on to turn the world upside down for Jesus.

It was a long process, but the disciples finally realized they had to place their trust in Jesus. They understood that their confidence was only as valid as its
source. If Jesus is your Savior, then you too have
hope for the future. Whatever might happen from
now till death, it doesn't really matter. Why? Because
you have placed your trust in a strong and mighty
Savior who has promised to strengthen you all the
days of your life and give you a future in heaven.

Take This Cup Away from Me

Jesus showed total resolve and confidence throughout the days
of His earthly ministry. He battled through the constant harass-
ment of the religious leaders in Israel. He battled through the spiritual immaturity of His men. Yet He never hesitated in His forward
movement toward the cross. But on the night that preceded His
betrayal, trial, and crucifixion, Jesus fought His own battle with
following through on the Father's will. How did He fight and win
this battle? He prayed, saying, "Father, if it is Your will, take this
cup away from Me; nevertheless not My will, but Yours, be done"
(Luke 22:42).

The confidence Jesus sought was there. The conflict was over
and the battle was won! Through long and agonizing prayer, Jesus'
anguish over His mission was resolved. His struggle was not with
God's will, but against the temptation to give in to the human emotion of fear. His resolve was restored, and His mission reaffirmed.

Doing God's will should always give you confidence
because it means you are doing the right thing. Unfortunately this also usually means you are doing the
most difficult tasks, the harder duties. As you survey the costs, whether physical, mental, or financial,

you may hesitate and think, *I'm not sure I want to do this or can do this. The price might be too high!* Just as Jesus experienced, there are times when you have a difficult and costly decision to make. During these crises, follow Jesus' example. Take your questions, fears, and reluctance to the Father in prayer. Reaffirm your willingness to do what's right in spite of your doubts. Then rise up...and do it! God will be honored and you will be blessed when you trust Him and do His will with full confidence.

You Shall Receive Power

The disciples often struggled with confidence. Perhaps their all-time low was fleeing in fear after the crucifixion. Later they came back and reassembled as they rallied around the risen Lord. But they were still hesitant and fearful, even to the time of Jesus' return to heaven. So, as a final confidence booster, Jesus made one last promise to the disciples before ascending into heaven: "You shall receive power when the Holy Spirit has come upon you; and you shall be witnesses to Me in Jerusalem, and in all Judea and Samaria, and to the end of the earth" (Acts 1:8).

When this promise came true and the Holy Spirit empowered the unsure disciples, they were completely transformed! They boldly preached the good news of Jesus' resurrection and thousands believed. It's no surprise that the religious leaders felt terribly threatened—so much so that they rounded up the disciples for interrogation. They were looking for some explanation for the power and confidence the disciples now possessed. And what was their conclusion? "As they observed the confidence of Peter and John and understood that they were uneducated and untrained men, they were amazed, and began to recognize them as having been with Jesus" (Acts 4:13 NASB).

We know what made a difference in the attitudes of the disciples, don't we? They went from being cowards to confident spokesmen of Christ. How did this happen? They had received the power of the Holy Spirit. It was the Spirit's confidence that empowered them. "And when they had prayed, the place where they were assembled together was shaken; and they were all filled with the Holy Spirit, and they spoke the word of God with boldness" (Acts 4:31).

The apostle Paul also realized the source of his confidence: "My speech and my preaching were not with persuasive words of human wisdom, but in demonstration of the Spirit and of power" (1 Corinthians 2:4). Paul's confidence was not in his privileged education, keen intellect, or his speaking ability, but in the knowledge that the Holy Spirit was energizing and guiding him.

Reflecting the Heart of Jesus

Confidence is a quality everyone desires and anyone can possess. You can take classes or receive special training to enable you to be more assertive, bold, and self-assured. Anyone can become more confident. But the confidence that comes from Christ and points to Him as its source is based on trust—trust in Him.

Are you placing your full trust in Jesus? Is your confidence at full strength, or have you lost sight of your identity with Christ? Are you confidently serving your family, raising your children, ministering your spiritual gifts, and being a bold witness with the authority of Christ? There is absolutely no reason for self-doubt or timidity. Redirect your focus to Jesus. You can have confidence in His absolute and unlimited authority. He is all you need for a bold confident life. Why? Because, as He explained to the disciples after His resurrection, "all authority has been given to Me in heaven and on earth" (Matthew 28:18). Go…with confidence!

～ A Prayer to Pray ～

Thank You, Lord Jesus, that You protect, sustain, and empower me for my many roles and responsibilities. Thank You that I can live and serve with confidence, knowing You are with me. And thank You for my future hope of dwelling with You forever in the house of the Lord. Great are You, Lord, and greatly to be praised! Amen.

Day 5

Courageous

*H*ow many situations arise in an "ordinary day" in your life that cause fear or doubt or a lack of confidence to well up in your stomach and maybe even up to your throat? I've made my own short list from some of my days that began in the usual way:

- Witnessing a teen boy and his dad in a physical and verbal brawl
- Enduring a super-bumpy plane ride
- Having a flat tire on a dark stretch of road at night
- Facing a public performance or ministry
- Suffering through a medical test to determine the cause of an illness
- Watching a grandchild suffer an unknown long-term medical condition
- Putting up with a stressful relationship with a family member

God has four words for us when we must face, endure, or are surprised by these kinds of challenges: "Do not be afraid" (Joshua 1:9). These words were spoken by God to Joshua, the new leader of the children of Israel, after Moses' death. Suddenly Joshua found himself responsible for leading a massive group of people—more than two million! It's no wonder that God had to encourage His new leader. Joshua was already a proven warrior who had fought many battles before receiving his new task. Yet God spent a considerable amount of time bolstering Joshua's courage and admonishing him about the dangers of fear (Joshua 1:1-9).

Fear is often seen as being reserved for the weak. But Joshua, a man experienced in warfare, was in no way weak. God knew Joshua, and He knows you and me too. He also knows that we are strong in many ways but still tend to have our own fears and doubts. But no worries! God told Joshua—and He speaks to us as well—to "be strong and of good courage." Why? Because "the LORD your God is with you wherever you go" (Joshua 1:9).

Reflecting On Your Heart

Step One to gaining courage is realizing that fear is natural, whereas the presence of God right beside you, all the time, is supernatural. When you recall this truth, you've successfully begun to fight your fears and gain strength and courage of heart for the tasks—and challenges—the Lord has prepared for you. Strength is yours when you remember that Jesus promised to stay with you when He said, "Lo, I am with you always, even to the end of the age" (Matthew 28:20).

Jesus Shows Us the Way

God was with Joshua infusing him with courage. And He's with you and me too. Today we consider a powerful character quality that was again perfectly modeled for us by Jesus. Jesus was courageous because He knew that He was in the faithful hands of the Father. Fear was never an issue for Jesus because He trusted in the Father's timetable for His life. This chapter—and this quality— is as much about trust as it is about bravery. If we trust that God will guide and protect us, then Jesus will provide the strength and courage we need to make it through the challenges of life...

...when your faith is put to the test.

...when you must hold the family together while your husband travels for his job or is deployed with the military.

...when you have a wayward child.

...when you or a loved one is facing a life-threatening illness or preparing to die.

Jesus was described as "a Man of sorrows" in Isaiah 53:3 because of the many burdens and sufferings He endured during His time on earth. He was exposed to the same types of potentially volatile situations as we are today, and He was victorious. That's why Jesus is the greatest model we can look to, observe, and emulate.

As women, we have great burdens to carry. Plus, we live in a world that's filled with suffering and is often scary. We're put into situations where we have to choose whether we will stand up, speak up, or live up to our calling as Christians...or not. But the good news is that Jesus offers us His courage for our daily living. Keep in mind as you read along that courage is bravery. It's the power to do something in the face of fear. It's also the ability to act on beliefs despite danger or disappointment. Courage also gives you great strength in the face of pain or grief.

He Drove Them All Out of the Temple

Jesus spoke about meekness, saying, "Blessed are the meek, for they shall inherit the earth" (Matthew 5:5). He also described Himself as "gentle and lowly in heart" (Matthew 11:29). And yet when Jesus saw the money changers in the temple, He "made a whip of cords, [and] He drove them all out of the temple...and poured out the changers' money and overturned the tables. And He said...'Do not make My Father's house a house of merchandise!'" (John 2:15-16).

It's true that God wants us, as His women, to have "a gentle and quiet spirit" (1 Peter 3:4). This God-pleasing attitude should be our constant desire. Under normal conditions as we go about living our days, meekness and a quiet spirit should be our demeanor. As you read the Gospels you see Jesus living in this same quiet, unhurried, relaxed spirit even in the midst of daily chaos. But on occasion we read that Jesus confronted religious hypocrites, defied man-made traditions, defended sinners, and denounced religious bigotry.

When Jesus cleared out the temple and confronted its leadership, He was angry because those who had come to worship at God's house were being exploited. He had an issue with how the leaders and merchants were abusing God's name, God's house, and God's people. He acted boldly with righteous indignation because of His authority as the Son of God.

In normal circumstances we want to display the same meekness and quiet spirit shown by Jesus. However, there may come times when we, like Him, need to be bold and courageous, to speak up. Maybe it's an issue with your child's school or church curriculum. Or maybe it's the person who's making false or ignorant statements about the Bible or Jesus. Or maybe some kind of abuse is occurring and you must confront a person or let officials know. These are the times when you need to summon the courage to stand up or speak up for what is right.

But here's a word of caution: You are not to use Jesus' example of righteous anger to justify your own selfish emotions and anger. It's right to be upset about injustices and sin, but it's wrong to be angry over trivial offenses or your personal soapbox issues. It's right to speak up when the character of God is slandered, but you are not to respond with hatred or violence. We are to obey the government and use lawful means to show our displeasure with unlawful or evil practices around us and in our community.

He Overcame the World

The night before His death, Jesus prepared His disciples for the trials He knew they would face. Just as Jesus reassured the Twelve, He also reassures you of His concern for you. When hard times come—and come they will—He will be there for you...and with you. The Lord will infuse you with His courage and strength as you trust Him. He will see you through any and all trouble because He is more powerful than any situation you will ever encounter. As He told His disciples, "These things I have spoken to you, so that in Me you may have peace. In the world you have tribulation, but take courage; I have overcome the world" (John 16:33 NASB).

Jesus was leaving this band of men. Together they had enjoyed constant fellowship for three years. Even though He had warned them previously of His departure, when "tribulation" came in the form of an arrest, a trial, and the cross, any courage they once had melted away. In fear, they deserted and denied Him. It wasn't until Jesus was raised from the dead and they were filled with His Spirit that courage became a dominant force in the disciples' lives.

===== *Reflecting On Your Heart* =====

Someday—maybe even today—you will need courage for the tribulations Jesus said will come your way. He encourages you in such times to be brave and trust in His promise, "I have overcome the world." This means He will be there with you, and He will provide all the courage you need for the moment.

His Soul Was Exceedingly Sorrowful

As you have already read, Jesus was preparing His disciples for His death. At last the time was drawing near for Him to die. What had been planned in eternity past was about to become reality. As in everything, Jesus prayed. He was in great anguish over His approaching physical pain, separation from the Father, and death for the sins of the world. The divine course was set, but the Son of God, in His human nature, still suffered, so much so that "His sweat became like great drops of blood falling down to the ground" as He uttered, "My soul is exceedingly sorrowful, even to death" (Luke 22:44; Matthew 26:38). Jesus battled the anguish of having to drink the full cup of the Father's divine fury against sin. But with the courage of divine resolve, He prayed, "My Father, if it is possible, let this cup pass from Me; yet not as I will, but as You will" (verse 39).

Obviously, you or I will never require the same level of courage and resolve that was needed for Jesus to drink God's cup of wrath against sin. But in our own difficulties in our own sphere, we too face times of great trial in body and spirit. Like Jesus, we want "this cup," whatever it might be, to pass from us. The pain and anguish seem too great to bear! But also, like Jesus, we want to glorify God and reflect Jesus' strong character in our trials. So, with broken hearts and trembling hands, we offer up our own prayer of "not as I will, but as You will" to our all-wise, sovereign, loving Father.

Others Who Show Us the Way

Most people spend their whole life building their reputation. Reputation is extremely important, and well it should be for us as Christians. But would you be willing to lose all that you've worked for if it meant standing up and doing the right thing to show your love for Jesus and your loyalty to the One who died for you? Look now at several examples of courage in those who took risks to follow Jesus.

The Women at the Cross

There are some women in the Bible I simply cannot point to enough because they were so courageous in their faithfulness to Jesus, no matter what. Be prepared—you'll meet up with them again in this book. They are the women who stayed with Jesus at the cross. They did the right thing in spite of the risks and the possibility of bodily harm and criticism from others.

Can you imagine the scene? The sky became dark even though it was still day. There were earthquakes with rocks splitting and tombs opening up, and many of the fallen saints of old rose from their graves. It was such a scary sight that even the hardened Roman soldiers "feared greatly" (Matthew 27:54). And all but one of Jesus' disciples fled this horrifying scene. Yet in the midst of these fearful and dangerous happenings we see that "many women who followed Jesus from Galilee, ministering to Him, were there looking on from afar" (verses 55-56).

These ladies were truly courageous when others feared and ran for their lives. "Why," you may be asking along with me, "were they so brave?" The answer is love—love for Jesus. Their love was so great and their faith was so strong that they fought off their fears and acted with courage.

> Faith in Jesus is always the antidote for fear. Our cour-
> age to fight off the fears of death, suffering, loss, or
> tragedy finds its strength in Jesus. So, again, when tri-
> als arrive, whatever they may be, look to Jesus. Let
> Him and His presence displace your fears with His
> courage. And count on His love. "The silver thread of
> God's love is woven into each of our trials."[2]

Fortunately, our opportunities to exhibit courage don't generally involve danger. But fear is always an element in suffering and
pain. That's why the example of these women is truly remarkable.
Their solution and the application of courage is the same for us.
Their faith in God empowered them with the bravery they needed
to face danger as they identified themselves with their Savior. They
were willing to stand up for Jesus and to serve Him to the very
end. Are you ready to make this kind of commitment? You can
always pray for God to strengthen your trust in Him and deepen
your love for Jesus. Do it daily so you will have the courage to
live for Jesus each and every day.

The Man Who Asked for the Body of Jesus

Joseph of Arimathea—Another person who found strength and
courage in Jesus was Joseph of Arimathea. He was a prominent
member of the council that judged Jesus and condemned Him to
death. Joseph, however, did not consent to the council's decision
(Luke 23:50-51). After witnessing the horrible tragedy of Jesus' unjust
death, he, along with Nicodemus, also a ruler of the Jews (John
3:1), decided to step forward and show their loyalty by taking care
of Jesus' burial (John 19:38-42).They were willing to—and probably did—lose all credibility with the other religious leaders of the
country for their actions.

Joseph and Nicodemus were secret believers…up to a point.
But no more! They looked up, manned up, stood up, spoke up,
and stepped up to take care of Jesus' body and burial. Remember their example and God's words to Joshua: "Be strong and of
good courage; do not be afraid" (Joshua 1:9).

Reflecting the Heart of Jesus

Jesus announced that "in the world you will have tribulation; but be of good cheer, I have overcome the world" (John 16:33). And He went on to urge His followers—including you—not to worry, because He will be with you. This fact, truth, and promise, all rolled into one, should bolster your courage.

Whether a tragedy or disaster or shock strikes during your day, and your heart sinks and you feel like your life is reeling and bewilderment sets in, you are never alone. In spite of the struggles you will experience, Jesus is always with you and will never abandon you. As He told His disciples before He left them, "Lo, I am with you always, even to the end of the age" (Matthew 28:20). Your precious, omnipresent Savior will go with you all the way through each trial…and all the way through life. The most effective and powerful way you can reflect the heart of Jesus is to entrust yourself into His capable hands. Let His confidence infuse you with the courage to face life boldly as you live in and for Jesus Christ. Because your ultimate victory has already been won by Christ, you can live in courage as you trust Him even in the worst of times.

~ A Prayer to Pray ~

Lord Jesus, I thank You that You are beside me right now and at all times. Help me to recall Your powerful presence when I need to be courageous and live boldly as a Christian, to speak up when it's the right thing to do, and stand up in the midst of difficult situations. Amen.

Disciplined

I can't believe it! My husband Jim wears the same jean size he wore in high school! Do you know anyone like that? (And does it make you mad?!) Some souls seem blessed to be able to eat anything they want, at any time. But a closer look reveals that in most cases these put-together people have a secret—they are disciplined. For instance, my Jim works out with weights, runs or walks an hour each day, weighs himself daily, and watches what he eats. With a few exceptions, most people who don't seem to have a weight problem are making sure it doesn't become a problem by nurturing and maintaining a disciplined lifestyle.

Now let me quickly say I'm mentioning the weight issue only because it's a personal problem and goal of mine. I could also easily point to gossip, erratic emotions, or chronic tardiness as areas that require discipline. But most of my friends and the women I know have difficulty with their weight. In fact, there's proof this is a problem for most people in America. The surgeon general's office considers excessive weight and obesity the number one health problem in the United States today. So what can we do? How can we have victory in this and all areas of life?

Jesus Shows Us the Way

Who do you think was the most disciplined person who ever lived? The section title above—and the focus of this book—has already given away the answer, hasn't it? It's Jesus. Being God in flesh, Jesus was in complete control at all times. He never allowed His mouth, emotions, or physical needs to get the best of Him. Today let's take note as we look at Jesus in all His perfect yet human discipline and self-control.

As we step into this all-important and difficult-to-obtain quality, consider the meaning of *discipline*. When spoken of as a fruit of the Spirit, discipline or self-control relates to curbing fleshly impulses (Galatians 5:22-23). In contemporary society, the general meaning of the word is "temperate." In the 1920s it was used to communicate the idea of temperance toward alcohol. Today, *discipline* can describe everything from living by a schedule to cleaning your house. (I recently read an article that reported that people who are physically disciplined are more likely to have a tidy house.) All in all, a disciplined person is able to master, control, curb, or restrain certain behaviors.

It Is Written...

As with each virtue, remember that Jesus was God yet He was human, possessing two natures that were never mingled. As a human, Jesus became what the Bible refers to as the "last" or second Adam (1 Corinthians 15:45). The first Adam was sinless until his fall into sin. The second Adam, Jesus, was sent by the Spirit into the wilderness to be tested and proven to be the Messiah, the Savior (Matthew 4:1-11). There He was relentlessly tempted by the devil for 40 days and 40 nights as He suffered thirst, starvation, and loneliness.

Yet Jesus did not yield to the devil's attempts to get Him to stop trusting God for His needs. Jesus remained faithful to God and fought off temptations by replying, "It is written..." (verses 4,7,10). With each enticement Jesus' defense against the devil's attack was Scripture. As God, Jesus could not sin, but the temptations were still real. For Him, the testing was necessary to validate His messiahship. Jesus' example shows us the way to attain discipline.

～ Look to Jesus' example: "For we do not have a High Priest who cannot sympathize with our weaknesses, but was in all points tempted as we are, yet without sin" (Hebrews 4:15).

~ Look to Jesus for help: "For in that He Himself has suffered, being tempted, He is able to aid those who are tempted" (Hebrews 2:18).

~ Look to Jesus through prayer: "Let us...come boldly to the throne of grace, that we may obtain mercy and find grace to help in time of need" (Hebrews 4:16).

───────── *Reflecting On Your Heart* ─────────

You too face dangerous and intense spiritual battles. When you're under some sort of pressure at work or at home, or you're suffering loss or illness, or even when you simply don't feel good, you are at great risk of spiritual attack. Many of these temptations come when you're alone with no one nearby to help. But take heart. You can call on God. You can tap into His power and His powerful Word for the discipline and self-control and the ammunition of scriptures you need to face temptation and be victorious.

He Departed to a Solitary Place

Maintaining discipline of any kind and for any purpose is difficult. But it seems (at least for me) like the spiritual disciplines are the most difficult to sustain. I constantly struggle with being faithful in spending time in prayer and in God's Word. But Jesus shows us the way to nurture these two spiritual disciplines...right down to a time and a place!

Scene 1—In this scene from Jesus' life, keep in mind that He wasn't on vacation or off on a spiritual retreat with time to kill or fill. You may recognize Mark 1:21-34 as a passage that describes one of the busiest days in Jesus' ministry life. He had done it all, teaching in a synagogue and healing just about everyone in the area. But rather than take the next day off, Mark reports that "in the morning, having risen a long while before daylight, He went out and departed to a solitary place; and there He prayed" (verse 35). Jesus got up early, before His disciples, and disappeared to a quiet place to pray. He chose to discipline Himself and do what He thought was most important—commune with the Father.

The Bible doesn't say how long Jesus prayed, but soon He would be bombarded with the ongoing needs of the people He had been with the day before. As Jesus was praying, "Simon and those who were with Him searched for Him. When they found Him, they said to Him, 'Everyone is looking for You'" (Mark 1:36-37).

The Bible also doesn't give us the content of Jesus' prayer, but it seems that He was seeking direction for the new day. The disciples, however, wanted to capitalize on the positive results of the previous day's ministry, and why not? Why not enjoy and build on the success of that day? But Jesus had received other orders while praying, for "He said to them, 'Let us go into the next towns, that I may preach there also, because for this purpose I have come forth'" (verse 38).

While Jesus sought the Father in prayer, He was given guidance about how to spend the day in front of Him. Also, Jesus was disciplined and didn't let Himself get sidetracked from His mission. One key message from this passage of Scripture is that you should seek to discipline yourself and not get distracted by what's happening around you. If you believe God is guiding you in a certain direction, stay focused and keep to that direction.

Reflecting On Your Heart

Most believers encounter a long list of difficulties when it comes to sustaining the disciplines of prayer and Bible reading. But Jesus shows us the way to ensure these two spiritual disciplines are a part of each day. First and foremost, He *desired* to communicate with the Father. He longed to discover and do His will. That was paramount. Therefore He *disciplined* Himself and got up. He didn't have someone else wake Him. Instead, He made the effort to get up and go to a place to pray. It was His choice. And He knew it was important enough to merit getting up before everyone else, before daybreak, to pray. Maintaining spiritual disciplines is a choice. You choose to do what you believe is important. Prayer was important to Jesus. Therefore He prayed. As a saying reminds us, "Prayer is the key of the morning and the bolt of the night." Use the reliable key of prayer to start your day with the Father and put yourself on His path. Then close your day in the same way and "lie down in peace, and sleep" (Psalm 4:8).

He Rebuked Them

Scene 2—Jesus was on His way to Jerusalem to fulfill the ultimate goal of His mission—to die as a sacrifice for sin (Luke 9:53-56). The most direct route was through Samaria. There was a long-standing fued between the Jews and the Samaritans, and normally Jewish travelers avoided Samaria at all costs. But on this occasion Jesus led His disciples through Samaria. Given the animosity between the two people groups, it isn't surprising that Jesus and His men were not given a cordial reception.

When brothers James and John heard that a Samaritan village had refused to offer basic hospitality to Jesus and their fellow disciples, they were furious. They immediately asked, "Lord, do You want us to command fire to come down from heaven and consume them, just as Elijah did?" (Luke 9:54). I'm not sure whether they could have actually called down fire or not, but their choice of words reveals their attitude. They were so mad that if they had possessed the power, they might have followed through and destroyed the entire village. These brothers loved Jesus and wanted to avenge the snub against Him. What was Jesus' response to their suggestion? "He turned and rebuked them, and said, 'You do not know what manner of spirit you are of'" (verse 55).

Reflecting On Your Heart

How do you respond to rebuffs? And what's your manner of spirit when you are brushed off? Do you jump onto an emotional roller coaster (like James and John did)? Or do you seek to control your emotions? As you walk by Jesus' Spirit, you will be able to control yourself and model Jesus and His self-control.

Others Show Us the Way

There are scores of people in the Bible I could point out to illustrate discipline...or a lack of it. But as a woman, I always look first to the women of the Bible. Meet two of them now. I'm sure you'll see some of yourself in each one, and maybe receive some pointers for any changes you need to make.

Blessed Is Your Discernment

Abigail shows us an example of discipline—She was, on all counts, an amazing woman. (You can read about her in 1 Samuel 25.) At a time when everyone else was out of control, Abigail demonstrated the powerful impact a woman can have when she shows discipline in the key areas of life. In stark contrast, Abigail's husband, Nabal, was arrogant, foolish, and a drunkard. David, the future king of Israel, had just reacted with anger when Nabal refused to give him payment for protecting Nabal's property.

In the midst of this explosive scene, Abigail responded with disciplined speech and behavior. She showed great wisdom and self-control. She stepped in and defused David's anger and diverted a life-threatening situation and potential bloodbath. This is David's praise of Abigail: "Blessed is the LORD God of Israel, who sent you this day to meet me! And blessed is your advice ['discernment,' NASB] and blessed are you, because you have kept me this day from coming to bloodshed and from avenging myself with my own hand" (1 Samuel 25:32-33).

She Took of Its Fruit and Ate

Eve shows us an example of a lack of discipline—unfortunately negative examples are often useful for teaching us how not to behave! And wouldn't you know, our negative example is Eve, the first woman who failed in the discipline department. When it came to the temptation to sin, she was weak, willful, and wanton. (See Genesis 3 for the whole sad story.) When Eve encountered the serpent, she listened too much to his lies. And she talked too much to this master deceiver. And she desired too much when offered the forbidden fruit. So "she took of its fruit and ate" (Genesis 3:6).

On the other side of "too much," Eve sought too little advice from God and from her husband. Rather than live out God's plan for her life, Eve rushed headlong into sin on every front. Rather than discipline her mouth, her mind, and her body, she acted sinfully and foolishly. Her willful actions—along with those of Adam—plunged mankind into sin. Only God's intervention in sending His only Son, the Lord Jesus, could undo what her lack of discipline created.

Things to Remember About Discipline

Discipline is a spiritual issue—Self-control is a manifestation of Jesus' Spirit at work in you (Galatians 5:22-23).

Discipline is affected by disobedience—Disobedience grieves and quenches the power of the Spirit's fruit of self-control in you (Ephesians 4:30; 1 Thessalonians 5:19).

Discipline is an act of the will—The Holy Spirit will not force you to be disciplined. You decide whether you will or won't walk by the Spirit. The Spirit of Jesus, however, prompts, moves, impresses, and convicts you of error (John 16:8), but He will not force you to live a godly life.

Discipline involves the whole woman—

Your emotions—"Whoever has no rule over his own spirit is like a city broken down, without walls" (Proverbs 25:28).

Your mouth—"Even a fool is counted wise when he holds his peace; when he shuts his lips, he is considered perceptive" (Proverbs 17:28).

Your eating—"Put a knife to your throat if you are a man [woman] given to appetite" (Proverbs 23:2).

Your diligence—"Do not love sleep, lest you come to poverty; open your eyes, and you will be satisfied with bread" (Proverbs 20:13).

Reflecting the Heart of Jesus

It's time for a look in the mirror. As you pause to consider your heart, ask: Do I want my life to make a difference? Do I want to live for God? Do I desire to positively influence those in my family, my circle of friends, my church, my workplace, and my community? If so, then following Jesus' example and living a more disciplined life is the answer and the way. To reflect Jesus and live out His purposes, embrace discipline as an essential element. Don't be like Eve, who failed to follow God because of a lack of self-control. Follow Abigail's excellent example of discipline in both word and deed. Then you will become a walking model of the disciplined behavior your Savior displayed.

~ A Prayer to Pray ~

Lord Jesus, I do want to be more disciplined, to live under the Spirit's control. May I seek to live a pure life, to be devoted to walking by Your Spirit in self-control. May discipline become a reigning quality in my life so You are glorified. Amen.

Day 7

Faithful

I've always admired the women who followed Jesus on His last journey from Galilee to Jerusalem. I've studied their stories, marveling at their closeness and familiarity with my Savior whom I long to see. This loyal band of ladies traveled with Jesus on many occasions and supported Him in a variety of ways. They were even present with Jesus the day of His crucifixion and death.

Can you even imagine what that last day in Jesus' life was like?! It was the most horrible day ever on earth. Yet these dear women were seen at the foot of the cross. They experienced the unnatural darkness that occurred (Luke 23:44) and witnessed the agony of Jesus' suffering, along with the mocking and jeering of the crowd and the savageness of the soldiers, all aimed at the lovely, sinless Son of God.

It seems like all of the horror and brutality and inhumane treatment would be more than a person could bear. Well, we know for sure that the disciples couldn't handle it! They all fled...except John. But these women didn't budge. In fact, after Jesus' death they went to His tomb to ensure He received a proper burial, only to find the tomb empty. Nothing—I repeat, *nothing*—kept these ladies from fulfilling what they considered to be their faithful duty to a friend, to Jesus.

As we begin another day of looking at the life and heart of Jesus and the qualities He consistently exhibited, we come to faithfulness—the virtue of loyalty, of being loyal and trustworthy. And what a powerful example of faithfulness we see displayed in the small band of women who knew and served the Son of God.

Where did these ladies find the strength and courage to be so loyal and faithful, especially under such trying circumstances? They had followed Jesus for some time, observing His life up close and personal, including this quality of faithfulness lived out in Him. They followed Him physically...and they followed His example of faithfulness to the point that they too became faithful in their to-the-end and no-matter-what service and support of His ministry (Luke 8:3). Ultimately their faithfulness enabled them to accompany Him to the cross and beyond!

With the memory of these remarkable women fresh in your mind, consider *faithfulness* and how it's developed. And before we look at how Jesus shows us the way, consider the faithfulness of the Father. From the opening pages of your Bible you can't help but notice:

⁓ He was faithful to provide coverings for Adam and Eve after their disobedience (Genesis 3:21).

⁓ He was faithful to promise a Savior (Genesis 3:15).

⁓ He was faithful to expand on His initial promise to send a Savior (Isaiah 9:6).

⁓ He was faithful in fulfilling His promise as Jesus, the God-man, God's only Son, was born as Savior (Luke 2:11).

⁓ He was faithful in providing a divine model of His very nature through the life and ministry of Jesus as He walked among us as God in human flesh (John 1:14).

Jesus Shows Us the Way

Following in His Father's holy footsteps, Jesus' life on earth gives us a firsthand example of faithfulness.

I Have Finished the Work

Jesus was faithful to God's purpose. He came to earth for a purpose, declaring, "My food is to do the will of Him who sent Me, and to finish His work" (John 4:34). Jesus' work was to live and die as the perfect sacrifice for man's sin. But as Jesus went about doing good and feeding the multitudes who followed Him from place to place, a groundswell formed. The people had a different purpose in mind for Jesus, especially after they witnessed Him feeding 5000-plus men and possibly their families. They wanted Him to be their leader and to provide food for them on a regular basis (John 6:26).

But despite the distractions and the appeals of the people, Jesus remained faithful to God's plan and defined it to the crowds by saying, "I have come down from heaven, not to do My own will [or, by the way, the will of the crowd], but the will of Him who sent Me. This is the will of the Father who sent Me, that of all He has given Me I should lose nothing, but should raise it up at the last day" (John 6:38-39).

To the very end, day by day Jesus faithfully moved toward the objective that had been set before Him by the Father. He stated His final assessment of His mission to His Father in a prayer given on the eve of His death: "I have glorified You on the earth. I have finished the work which You have given Me to do" (John 17:4).

I don't know about you, but it's extremely easy to get distracted from God's calling on my life. This person wants me to do this, and another wants me to do that. I'm pulled in all different directions at once! And then there are those days I'm not sure I really want to do *any*thing! Do you ever feel like this? Well, maybe the reason for the distractions and misdirection is that we don't know our true purpose in life...or haven't reviewed it in a while. Therefore, we find ourselves trying to ride off in all directions at once—or doing nothing!

What does God want you and me to do with our lives? If you don't have a good understanding about it—or even a clue, read Titus 2:3-5 for a few hints. As these verses suggest, it helps to seek out an older woman to give you some guidance and direction and to assist you in clarifying and polishing up God's purpose for you.

=== *Reflecting On Your Heart* ===

You may already be pursuing God's purpose, but as a follow-up, you might also want to ask yourself, Am I faithfully serving those in my path who are part of my purpose—my family, my church, my co-workers and acquaintances? Am I willing to follow in Jesus' faithful steps and make the sacrifices faithfulness requires? Growing more like Jesus awaits you on the other side of these answers and actions.

Pray and Do Not Lose Heart

Jesus was also faithful in prayer. One of the most amazing aspects of Jesus' incarnation, His coming as a man, is the fact that He voluntarily submitted Himself to the control of the Holy Spirit. Prayer was a key medium by which He communicated with the Father and received direction. Jesus lived in the spirit of prayer. He could be alone with the Father in the midst of a pressing crowd or while without another single person in a secluded place. Prayer was His life, His habit. He prayed in every situation, in every emergency, and at every opportunity for all issues. For instance,

- He prayed in the midst of a busy life. Most people stress out under the pressure of a busy life. But not our Lord. He had another way of dealing with the pressure of one hectic day after another. What was His secret? After a hugely successful—and harried—day of ministry, we see that the next morning, instead of celebrating His success, Jesus rose "a long while before daylight...went out and departed to a solitary place; and there He prayed" (Mark 1:35).

- He prayed before and during important events, particularly His impending death on the cross (Matthew 26:39-42).

- He prayed for others. Intercession for others was a dominant feature in His prayers. (For a divine example, read through His "High Priestly Prayer" in John 17.)

- He prayed for His enemies. "Father, forgive them, for they do not know what they do" (Luke 23:34).

You cannot read very far in the Gospels without sensing the

importance of prayer in the life of Jesus. He faithfully taught all who listened that they "always ought to pray and not lose heart" (Luke 18:1). His commitment to faithful prayer is calling you and me to diligently and purposefully nurture the habit of prayer.

Those Whom You Gave Me I Have Kept

Jesus was faithful to His disciples too. Loyalty is a rare quality, both today and in Jesus' day. Jesus' disciples were simple men—fishermen for the most part. They were unsophisticated, naive, and oblivious to the evil intents of the religious leaders. While they were physically with Jesus, He steadfastly protected them and kept them safe from the world. As Jesus attested to the Father in prayer on the eve of His death, "while I was with them in the world, I kept them in Your name. Those whom You gave Me I have kept; and none of them is lost except the son of perdition, that the Scripture might be fulfilled" (John 17:12).

This promise continues on for you and all who put their faith and trust in Jesus (John 10:28-29). Jesus again models the quality of faithfulness when He acknowledged that the Father had given Him charge of the disciples as His stewardship: "I have manifested Your name to the men whom You have given Me out of the world. They were Yours, You gave them to Me" (John 17:6).

═══════════════ *Reflecting On Your Heart* ═══════════════

Do you realize that God has also given you a "charge" in the lives of all your family members and in the use of your spiritual gifts? God asks for your faithfulness with these precious lives and gifts. As 1 Corinthians 4:2 says, "It is required in stewards that one be found faithful."

Honor Your Father and Your Mother

And speaking of family, Jesus was faithful to His family. Luke's Gospel states that Jesus did not begin His ministry until He was about 30 years old (Luke 3:23). Can you imagine how patient (another quality we'll consider) God in flesh had to be to wait until He was 30? A Jewish boy was considered a man at about age 12. So what did Jesus do during all those years of waiting? The Bible doesn't say, but as the eldest son, it would have been Jesus' responsibility to care for the family if or when Joseph died. Jesus probably faithfully cared for His mother and half brothers and sisters until some of the boys were old enough to assist in the support of the family.

Even to the end, Jesus did not abandon Mary, His mother. Looking down from the cross upon His mother and John, the disciple whom Jesus loved, He uttered, "'Woman, behold your son!' Then He said to the disciple, 'Behold your mother!' And from that hour that disciple took her to his own home" (John 19:26-27).

Jesus said to "honor your father and your mother" (Matthew 15:4). And He modeled how honor is fleshed out. Jesus showed us in the last hours of His life how important our families are. He showed love and respect for His mother by faithfully consigning her into the care of John. And we are to show the same kind of care. We are to see our families as important—not only our husband and children, but our parents and yes, even our in-laws!

Reflecting the Heart of Jesus

As a Christian woman it is vital that faithfulness be a quality that shines brilliantly in your life. Why? Because this quality reflects Jesus to others. When you're faithful, you show that you are born of God and belong to Him through His Son. Jesus had a heart for the Father and doing His will. He had a heart for others and praying for them. And He had a heart for family and caring for them.

As you walk in faithfulness, you mirror the heart of your steadfast Savior. You also bear fruit in the lives of those you come in contact with. Your family is blessed because of your constant care. Your church benefits from your committed use of your spiritual gifts. And if you hold down a job, your boss and fellow employees profit from your fidelity.

We've marveled at many instances of Jesus' faithfulness. And the good news is you can nurture and develop this same sterling quality. You can grow in faithfulness that follows through, delivers the goods, shows up, keeps her word and her commitments, and is devoted to duty. And if this sounds impossible or like a hard uphill road, take courage! Step One? Call upon God in prayer. And start small—in the little things. Count on Jesus' strength too. In Him you can do all things, including being faithful (Philippians 4:13). And ask God for His enabling grace to work at eliminating laziness and fulfilling one of His purposes for you—that you would be "faithful in all things" (1 Timothy 3:11).

Our great, faithful God has already made available to you all that you require to be faithful. He has given you the Helper, the Holy Spirit. He has given you His Word, the Bible, to serve as a guide. And, praise upon praise, He has given you Jesus as a living model of faithfulness. Jesus lived it out day by day, minute by minute, incident by incident...and you can too. In our Savior's words, "He who is faithful in what is least is faithful also in much" (Luke 16:10). Once again, start small, for faithfulness in a little thing is a great thing.

～ A Prayer to Pray ～

Lord Jesus, may I day by day walk by Your Spirit so faithfulness is reflected in my life. May my love and service be steadfast. May I stand before You when my days on earth are done and hear You say, "Well done, good and faithful servant." This, dear Jesus, is my heart's desire. Amen.

Day 8

Focused

ince my preteen years, when my parents gave me a diary with its own lock and key, I've kept a journal. Over the years this practice led to noting and saving dates to remember.

To this day, I have certain dates I transfer each year to my new calendar. Of course, those dates include my wedding anniversary and birthdays of family members, even the dates when Jim and I moved to a new home or location. And then there is the monumental date—the day I became a Christian!

But there's one other date that was utterly life-changing: August 21, 1974. It was just another Sunday afternoon. But on this particular one Jim and I sat down together while our little ones napped, and we each wrote some significant lifetime goals. We had been a Christian family for only a few years, and we were loving our new journey with Jesus. We were still excited, but felt that we needed to get a better focus on this amazing new life in Christ. You see, we were all over the map in our enthusiasm to serve our Savior. So we prayed for God's wisdom and guidance, and went about setting some general and specific goals for our growth, our family, and our service to God.

From those few hours on a lazy Sunday afternoon we formulated a set of goals that we've each operated by for more than 30 years. I have to admit, my goals have never changed. As we defined our purposes and wrote out our objectives, we began to simplify our focus in life and whittle down our activities to fit into the targeted areas. As I said, these many years later we are still focused on our original goals and living daily with these same purposes guiding us.

Jesus Shows Us the Way

"Aim at nothing and you will hit it every time." Have you heard that quip? Well, aimlessness is what living without focus produces. You wake up each day and head off in all directions at once. But as you and I come to another day in our journey with Jesus, we want to camp a while on this next exemplary quality in Jesus—His focus. We are treated to a look at Someone (and that's with a capital S!) whose life was lived with and for a purpose. How did Jesus fulfill His purpose? To answer this question, let's look to Jesus and four prominent features that marked His days. He shows us the way as He moves through a handful of practices that contributed to the fulfillment of His mission. You and I can follow these same practices as well so that we also live our days with focus.

Jesus Himself Began His Ministry

Jesus prepared—One of my favorite principles for daily living and purpose is this: "Success is when preparation meets opportunity." Preparation is a necessary step in living out God's purpose. It gives you the ability to seize opportunities as they present themselves later in the day...or in life.

Whenever I teach on planning and preparation, I use Jesus as the ultimate illustration. He spent almost 30 years preparing for the day when He began His ministry. The same was true of Jesus' cousin, John the Baptist, who prepared for 30 years for his one-year ministry of heralding the coming of Messiah. These two men's paths crossed at the Jordan River, where John was baptizing people and Jesus showed up to be baptized. Immediately after His baptism, Jesus began His three years of earthly ministry: "Now Jesus Himself began His ministry at about thirty years of age" (Luke 3:23).

Formally, it was at age 30 that Jesus began His public ministry to fulfill His purpose. But He didn't wait until age 30 to prepare to minister. He had been doing that for three decades. And He didn't wait 30 years to bless and serve others because we know

He served His family at home. And you and I shouldn't wait to serve others either. While we're preparing by gaining knowledge, skills, and developing our spiritual gifts, we can serve in a multitude of ways, beginning right at home.

That's what happened in my life and how my ministry began. It took seven years of spiritual growth and directed study—seven years of preparation—before I taught my first Bible study. During those seven years I devoted myself to raising my children, supporting my busy husband, and striving to grow in my Christian walk. Then one day, when my children were older and in school, I was invited to teach a workshop to a small group of ladies. I prayed and then hesitantly said yes. Well, the abbreviated version of my story is that for 20-plus years I taught a variety of women's Bible studies at my church and, in God's timing, that teaching ministry developed into a writing ministry.

I want to quickly say this is what happened in *my* life. God works in different ways through His people. I could write pages about what happened in the lives of my friends and other women at my church and still others I've met over the decades. Teaching is not my point here, nor is it necessarily to be your goal. No, preparing yourself is the point! As you read the Word, grow spiritually, seek God's direction through prayer, and serve God's people, certain gifts or services will rise to the top. You may find yourself giving out advice or counsel. Or flinging open your doors in hospitality. Or organizing conferences or leading a committee. Or giving your time and money to a worthy ministry or mission. Or taking the elderly to doctors' appointments and leaving a special meal with them. As the Bible says, "There are diversities of gifts...differences of ministries...diversities of activities" (1 Corinthians 12:4-6). As you prepare yourself through spiritual growth, you will be preparing yourself for your unique contribution to the body of Christ.

―――――― *Reflecting On Your Heart* ――――――

To live with purpose means to focus your heart, time, energies, and priorities. It calls for aggressively taking advantage of each day, not only to help others, but also to prepare for future ministry. Then when clear avenues of service present themselves, you'll find yourself ready. What can you do today to prepare for the opportunities that are awaiting you? Write it down and pray over it. Then do it. Your daily focus on preparation will bring new energy and progress to your day.

While He Prayed...

Jesus prayed—As Jesus began His ministry, we see Him praying. The prayer He lifted up right after His baptism is often overlooked. Luke is the only writer of the four Gospels who tells us what happened: "When all the people were baptized, it came to pass that Jesus also was baptized; and while He prayed, the heaven was opened" (Luke 3:21).

We cannot hear too often about the importance of prayer and purpose as modeled by Jesus. Jesus was in constant fellowship with the Father. In this book we see Him praying before events (before choosing the 12 disciples—see Luke 6:12), praying at events (at the Last Supper—see John 17), or praying for an upcoming event (for His trial and death—see Luke 22:40-46).

Reflecting On Your Heart

Is God's purpose for you firmly fixed in your heart and mind yet? Be sure to look to Jesus and allow Him to serve as your perfect model for knowing God's plan, for focusing on it, and living it out. As you steadily make prayer a habit, you will discover God's plan for your life unfolding as He leads you. As you pray, your days will become pointed rather than pointless, full rather than empty, hopeful rather than hopeless, vibrant rather than vacant.

He Chose Us in Him

Jesus planned—As a member of the Godhead, the Son, along with the Father, made this plan in eternity past: "He chose us in

Him before the foundation of the world, that we should be holy and without blame before Him in love, having predestined us to adoption as sons by Jesus Christ to Himself, according to the good pleasure of His will" (Ephesians 1:4-5).

Obviously you and I benefitted from God's plan! Aren't you glad there was a plan? And you and I need to plan too if we're going to focus on fulfilling God's purposes and bless others. His purpose for you will take your lifetime to complete. If you try to look ahead at your whole life all at once, you'll probably feel overwhelmed. But if you break down your goals and desires into smaller bits and pieces and focus on them, you'll find them easier to manage. This is where scheduling comes to the rescue. When you make a schedule for each day, you can slot in one or two more steps toward your goals. With a plan and a schedule in your hand and your heart, you can then move on to the next phase of accomplishing God's purpose: You can proceed!

He Steadfastly Set His Face to Go to Jerusalem

Jesus proceeded—We can make plans all day long, but until we move out in action to make those plans a reality, it's just talk and dreams. The day arrived when Jesus knew that His time on earth was just about over. He would soon die and return to heaven. Therefore, it was time to proceed and fulfill the purpose of His coming to earth. "When the time had come for Him to be received up...He steadfastly set His face to go to Jerusalem" (Luke 9:51). It was time for Jesus to die and "give His life a ransom for many" (Matthew 20:28).

Although Jesus knew He would face humiliation and death at the hands of godless sinners when He got to Jerusalem, He was determined to go there. Knowing His purpose gave Jesus further resolve to proceed and complete the task given to Him by the Father.

===== *Reflecting On Your Heart* =====

Purpose or focus is all about getting ready to do God's will. Jesus was determined to proceed to Jerusalem in spite of what He knew was waiting for Him. He models the kind of resolve that should characterize your life too. Think about your level of determination. Are you focused…or easily diverted from God's purpose for you? Distraction is around every corner when His plan isn't clearly fixed in your mind. God has sovereignly given you a course of action. Hopefully, you have it firmly fixed in your heart and mind—and schedule—and are steadily proceeding toward it, toward fulfilling God's purpose, no matter what obstacles may await you.

The Angels Ministered to Him

The Father provided—Now may I quickly add a PS to my last sentence? It goes without saying, but here's a reminder: God's purpose for your life will not come without His provision in at least two areas. This was true in Jesus' case as well.

THE FATHER'S PROVISION FOR TEMPTATION

As God, Jesus couldn't sin, but the intensity of each temptation He faced was severe. During those times when Jesus was under extreme physical duress, the Father provided angelic support.

The first was during 40 days of testing by Satan while Jesus was deprived of food and water. "He was there in the wilderness forty days, tempted by Satan, and was with the wild beasts; and the angels ministered to Him" (Mark 1:13).

The other was in the Garden of Gethsemane, where Jesus wrestled with His purpose: "Then an angel appeared to Him from heaven, strengthening Him. And being in agony, He prayed more earnestly. Then His sweat became like great drops of blood falling down to the ground" (Luke 22:43-44).

In the midst of the agony of these two temptations to relinquish trust in the Father, the Father provided for His Son. Angels were sent to minister to Jesus and strengthen Him.

God has also made provision for you and me as well in the area of temptation. He has a plan for you. And He knows sin can hinder the fulfillment of that plan. So, as the apostle Paul explains,

"God is faithful, who will not allow you to be tempted beyond what you are able, but with the temptation will also make the way of escape, that you may be able to bear it" (1 Corinthians 10:13).

────────── *Reflecting On Your Heart* ──────────

"God is faithful." Let this truth refresh your heart! God will not always remove your temptations because they make your faith in Him stronger as you resist. However, He does promise to keep the temptation from becoming so strong that you can't stand up under it. Whatever you do, don't try to deal with your temptations alone. Through prayer, the assistance of God's Word, and support from others, God provides the way for you to remain faithful when you are tempted. Count on it!

THE FATHER'S PROVISION FOR ALL LIFE'S NEEDS

Paul had an "in" with God, a personal relationship with His Son, the Lord Jesus. Therefore, Paul was able to give you and me a promise of God's provision. He wrote, "My God shall supply all your need according to His riches in glory by Christ Jesus" (Philippians 4:19). If Jesus is your personal Savior, you, along with all believers, have this promise of provision for all your real needs. You can always count on God to supply all that is required to sustain you.

────────── *Reflecting On Your Heart* ──────────

Think about it. God has provided for all your needs. What a magnificent promise! He has a purpose for you, and you can move toward fulfilling it without fear or anxiety because of His guaranteed 100 percent provision. Whatever your need is today, whether it's financial, physical, emotional, or spiritual, boldly take that need to God. Then stand back and behold as the Father helps you fulfill your purpose by supplying all your needs according to His riches in glory by and because of His Son, Jesus.

God's Word Shows Us the Way

It's difficult for us as Christian women to know our purpose. There are so many voices shouting at us, suggesting all kinds of goals for us. But God's Word makes our purpose completely clear. His voice rises majestically above the clamor of the opinions and advice others have for you and me...and anyone else who will listen. And the good news is that God doesn't ask a thousand or even a hundred things of His women. He only asks us to focus on ten things, ten essentials that help us fulfill His grand purpose for us as women who love Him, who love and serve others, and who reflect Him to the world. His list, found in Titus 2:3-5, contains these essentials for us to focus our time and energies on:

1. Be godly in your behavior.

2. Be truthful and kind in your speech.

3. Be disciplined and self-controlled.

4. Be a teacher and encourager of good things.

5. Be devoted to your husband.

6. Be devoted to your children.

7. Be discreet and wise in your actions.

8. Be chaste and pure inside and out.

9. Be focused on your home.

10. Be kind and good to all.

Reflecting the Heart of Jesus

It's profoundly liberating to know your purpose in life. To drift aimlessly through your precious days is tiresome, frustrating, and unrewarding. It would be a great tragedy to wake up one day and realize all you could have accomplished if you had focused on some worthy goals along the way. You may already know your purpose. If so, focus your time and energies on it. But if you're a little behind or uncertain, spend time examining Jesus' life. Pay close attention to His focus and confidence as He lived God's purpose on a daily basis. Notice how He fixed His gaze on God's plan for Him. And be encouraged! As a woman who is seeking God's plan, you are already evidencing purpose. You are reflecting Jesus as you live out His instructions to "seek first the kingdom of God" (Matthew 6:33).

~ A Prayer to Pray ~

Blessed Jesus, I have so much to do…and want to do. And I have so many options today for how I spend my time and where I put my focus. My heart yearns to live for You and live out Your plan for me. Know my heart and lead the way. I want to follow! Amen.

Day 9

Forgiving

I forgive you." Three words. Three words that are somewhat easy to say. Three words that are extremely hard
to mean and live.

Since the day Adam and Eve succumbed to the wiles of the
devil in Genesis 3 and disobeyed God, sin has been a part of everyday life for every living being. You cannot go through even one
day without someone hurting you. You can be snubbed, ignored,
overlooked, or passed over. You can be told off, put down, and
berated. You can be betrayed and let down. You can be gossiped
about and slandered. You can be tricked, duped, and cheated. You
can be lied to, abused, or dumped as a friend, participant, partner,
or employee. And these offenses can also happen to your family
members and friends.

This list of injustices could go on and on...and it does! But our
focus as we consider what it means to reflect the heart of Jesus
needs to be this: Because mistreatment is a common, predictable,
for-certain occurrence, what can we do about it? What are we to
do with the pain inflicted upon us and our loved ones? How can
we bear the wrongs and yet forgive those who inflicted them? You
know, like Jesus did...and like Jesus told us to do? Or put another
way, How can we reflect Christ's magnificent forgiveness?

Jesus Shows Us the Way

Before we begin today's look at Jesus and His divine ability to forgive, let's take a look at the very origin of forgiveness for the human race by turning back the clock. Let's visit the scene I mentioned above that occurred in the Garden of Eden. What happened after Adam and Eve rebelled against God? Well, there were definite consequences. First, the couple was sentenced to a life of pain and hard labor, neither of which they had ever experienced in the sinless perfection of Eden. Then they were expelled from the garden paradise they had always known and thrust into a sin-laden world to fend and provide for themselves. That's the bad news.

But the good news is that God forgave the sinful couple He had lovingly created to have sweet, intimate, perfect fellowship with Him. Furthermore, He clothed them (Genesis 3:21) and sent them out to have a new life as opposed to the death their sin merited. Though their new home in the world was nothing as lovely and perfect as what they had experienced in the garden (verses 17-19), God provided for their needs.

Forgiveness back then began with God, and it still does today. God took the initiative to forgive Adam and Eve's sin. His first act of forgiveness and cleansing toward them was to clothe them with the skins of sacrificed animals. The physical deaths suffered by the animals should have been theirs, but it was the animals that died—a preview of Jesus' substitutionary death for our sins.

In this act of providing animal skins to cover the nakedness of the man and woman, the Almighty set up a system for forgiving the sins of His people. That system found its final sacrifice for the forgiveness of sin in the death of Jesus. Throughout the Bible God the Father refers to Himself as the God of forgiveness. And this forgiveness was modeled for us in the life and death of Jesus, God's Son.

Forgive That Your Father May Also Forgive You

You know what "normal" is, don't you? It's the response we instinctively leap to when we're hurt. Whether our injury is emotional or physical, we move into retaliation mode. Normal thinks, *You hurt me, so I'm gonna hurt you.* This kind of response is the natural, normal pattern of the world. It's no secret that forgiveness is not the normal or human response.

But Jesus shows us the way. In fact, He calls us to give the opposite response when we've been wronged. We're to reflect Jesus and give the *supe*rnatural response. Returning evil for evil is not how Jesus responded to the abuses heaped upon Him. He responded— and taught that we should respond—in the exact opposite way! He said, "Whenever you stand praying, if you have anything against anyone, forgive him, that your Father in heaven may also forgive you your trespasses" (Mark 11:25). With these words, Jesus Himself lets us know what He desires from us. (And by the way, these are not suggestions, but commands from the Master Himself.)

Jesus is asking you and me to forgive as He did—to reflect Him. He wants us to respond to a higher standard, a divine standard. Like the saying goes, "To err is human, but to forgive, divine." This means that if the person who hurts you or devastates your life never repents...or never acknowledges the pain caused to you... or never asks you for forgiveness...or never even says "I'm sorry," you are still willing to extend forgiveness. Forgiving that person will free you of a heavy burden of bitterness.

Reflecting On Your Heart

Forgiveness is not about "them." It's not about those who hurt you. It's about you and your connection with God. How is your relationship with Him? Have you accepted the death of Jesus in your place as forgiveness for your sins? Forgiving others begins with God. As a principle from Jesus teaches us, those who are forgiven much love much (Luke 7:47).

Love One Another

In forgiveness Jesus implemented a new order of living—living in love rather than hate. He was the pure embodiment of God's love, and commanded His disciples—and His followers from then on (that's you and me!)—to manifest that same love toward others. He said, "A new commandment I give to you, that you love one another; as I have loved you, that you also love one another. By this all will know that you are My disciples, if you have love for one another" (John 13:34-35).

Our Savior's plea, issued to us all those centuries ago, was to imitate His heart of forgiveness. As He pointed out, our love and forgiveness would be—and is—a sign to the watching world that we march to the beat of a different drum. We follow the Lord Christ, not our emotions, or what we see or read, or what we witness all around us or are told to do. When we love and forgive others as Jesus did, we shout to the world that we are God's children. Truly, forgiveness is a mark of Christian love.

Do Good to Those Who Hate You

No one can make you forgive another person. Forgiveness must come from the inside and work its way out into a physical response. Jesus knows your heart and He also knows that at times it's difficult in your heart to forgive those who have hurt you. So, as an act of your will, try responding with kind actions. Many times you will discover that right actions will lead to right feelings. Our Lord tells you to...

> love your enemies, do good to those who hate you, bless those who curse you, and pray for those who spitefully use you. To him who strikes you on the one cheek, offer the other also. And from him who takes away your cloak, do not withhold your tunic either. Give to everyone who asks of you. And from him who takes away your goods do not ask them back. And just as you want men to do to you, you also do to them likewise (Luke 6:27-31).

Reflecting On Your Heart

A pure heart filled with God's love will enable you to show love and forgiveness to someone who's wronged you. How is this done? You can extend kindness and goodness. You can give a helping hand. You can send a gift. You can smile at that person. Many times you'll discover that your first move will melt their coldness toward you. But regardless, you will have activated—or defrosted!—any coldness in your heart. You will be moving forward in forgiving a person who's wronged you. You'll find your heart melting so you can freely forgive another just as God in Christ has forgiven you (Ephesians 4:32).

Forgive Men Their Trespasses

I mentioned earlier that God commands us to forgive others. That means forgiveness is not optional. As Jesus communicates in what we refer to as the Lord's Prayer, we are to forgive "those who have wronged us" (Matthew 6:12).[3] Forgiving others is not up for debate. No, it is the very mark of a Christian. Jesus gives a startling warning about forgiveness: "If you forgive men their trespasses, your heavenly Father will also forgive you. But if you do not forgive men their trespasses, neither will your Father forgive your trespasses" (Matthew 6:14-15). If we expect to be forgiven, we need to practice forgiveness.

God's forgiveness of sin is not based on one's forgiving others. A Christian's forgiveness *is* based on realizing he has been forgiven (Ephesians 4:32). Daily and ongoing personal fellowship with God is in view in these verses (not salvation from sin). One cannot walk in fellowship with God if he refuses to forgive others.

How Often Should I Forgive?

One day while Jesus was teaching in the region around the Sea of Galilee, His disciple Peter asked a question that had probably been forming in his mind for some time. "Lord, how often shall my brother sin against me, and I forgive him? Up to seven times?" (Matthew 18:21). Peter was being generous when he suggested forgiving someone seven times, for the traditional rabbinic teaching was that an offended person needed to forgive a brother only three times. Peter had been around Jesus enough to know that forgiving others was important to the Lord. But perhaps he wondered, *When is enough enough?* And Peter was right to think that Jesus would probably want those who followed Him to show more forgiveness than rabbinic tradition required.

However, Jesus' reply communicated that we need to exercise forgiveness to a much greater extent. "I do not say to you, up to seven times, but up to seventy times seven" (verse 22). You can do the math—that's 490 times we're to forgive an individual who sins against us time and time again. By saying 70 times 7, Jesus was teaching that forgiveness is to be extended 490 times…plus! In other words, forgiveness has no limits. We're to forgive no matter what the number of sins committed! Jesus set no limits on our forgiving an individual who has committed limitless offences against us.

Then Jesus, the Master Teacher as well as the Master Forgiver, told a parable that illustrated the concept of unlimited forgiveness (verses 23-35). He told of a king who wanted to settle accounts with his servants. One servant owed an enormous amount—10,000 talents! This is the equivalent of about a million dollars in today's economy. Well, of course the servant couldn't pay. So, according to the custom of the day, the king ordered the servant and his family to be sold as slaves to recoup part of his debt. But when the servant pleaded with his master, begging for time to repay his debt, the master took pity on the servant, canceled the debt, and set him free.

So what did the forgiven debtor do? He went out and found another servant who owed him a much smaller amount—100 denarii, with each denarii being the equivalent of a day's wages. The first servant demanded payment and refused to show mercy toward his debtor. In fact, he had the second servant thrown into prison until he paid the debt.

How did the parable end? Other servants went to the master and told him what had happened, what his forgiven servant had done to a fellow servant. When the master heard this, he called back the first servant and jailed him for failing to show mercy to a fellow servant when he had been forgiven a much greater debt.

By way of this parable, Jesus was teaching that forgiveness should be in direct proportion to the amount we've been forgiven. The first servant had been forgiven all, and he in turn should have forgiven all. If you are a child of God, all your sins have been forgiven through faith in Jesus Christ. Therefore, when someone sins against you, you are to forgive that person fully from your heart, no matter how many times the act occurs.

Father, Forgive Them

Are you wondering, *Is there any action that is too great for forgiveness?* Once again Jesus' own gracious, loving, forgiving life shows us the answer—and the way. Our dear precious Savior demonstrated the ultimate in forgiveness. It occurred on the bleakest, darkest day in all history—the day Jesus was crucified. Picture the sinless Lamb of God, who went about doing good for over three years of earthly ministry. Because of His kindness, the deaf could hear, the blind could see, the dead were raised, and sinners were forgiven. And yet we tearfully end the reading of each of the four Gospels trying to contemplate our Jesus, God in human flesh, hanging on a cross and suffering the most inhumane of deaths.

How did Jesus respond to the cruelty inflicted on Him? He said, "Father, forgive them, for they do not know what they do" (Luke 23:34). These almost unbelievable words were an expression of the limitless compassion of divine grace.

Let's consider the question again: Is any action too great for forgiveness? In our Lord we have our answer, don't we? We don't even need to ask the question. We need only to look to Jesus. His ultimate act of forgiveness is not only the instruction but the example we need to move us to extend this same grace and compassion to those who inflict far less pain and heartache. Jesus never asks anything of us He did not do Himself. He asks us to forgive. He expects us to forgive. And He enables us with the power and ability to forgive. By His all-sufficient grace, you can forgive!

Reflecting the Heart of Jesus

What confidence is yours when you know that you are forgiven in Christ! That forgiveness of sin produces life everlasting, which you began participating in from the moment of salvation. When Christ is your Savior, God's Holy Spirit comes to reside in you. That means you can exhibit Christlike behavior (Galatians 5:22-23).

Here's how it works. Christ in you enables you to reflect Christlike character. For instance, it allows you to be "longsuffering" or to show "patience" (NASB). Longsuffering or patience refers to your ability to endure injuries inflicted by others and your willingness to accept annoying or painful situations. In Christ you are capable of not only withstanding great pain and suffering inflicted by others, but you also possess the strength and power of Christ to forgive—with His love—those who cause the hurt.

~ A Prayer to Pray ~

Lord Jesus, thank You for forgiving my sin, and help me in turn to forgive others. Search my heart for situations in which I'm not fully forgiving a wrong inflicted upon me. Whenever I recall the injury, pain, or memory of that hurt, let the beauty of Your forgiveness wash over me. Give me the love to forgive seventy times seven. Amen.

Generous

*B*elieve it or not, as much as Jim and I are on the go, I'm not a big fan of travel, especially international trips. I don't have many fond memories of marathon plane rides. What I do remember are the concerns Jim and I have when we land in Sao Paulo or Bangkok or wherever for an important ministry commitment, and we wonder if our luggage arrived with us or if it took its own separate journey to Berlin or Beijing.

On one such occasion, the two of us arrived in a Caribbean country for a ministry conference...only to discover that our bags had indeed taken a trip to an entirely different Caribbean country. But this seeming disaster was the beginning of a most incredible display of Christlike generosity. As soon as we landed we were informed that the wife of the president of the country had invited us to the presidential palace to meet with her. From that moment our hosts began to give liberally to us—literally the shirts off their own backs...and their shoes too! They gave us everything we needed to get us ready for an audience with a powerful leader's wife! And as I said, that was just the beginning of a weekend of abounding generosity.

To this day, whenever I think of generosity, these dear folks come to mind. As I recall their grace in giving so much to us, I stop and think, *This is so like Jesus, our Savior, who was Himself generous beyond imagination.* A giving heart like the one exhibited by our new friends in a foreign country should be the norm, but sadly, that's not often enough the case. Maybe that's why Christlike generosity is such a shock when it's offered.

Jesus Shows Us the Way

It's a new day in our journey into the character of Jesus. And, once again, we are privileged to look at His exemplary life. Without question, He is the ultimate model of generosity, for He gave the ultimate gift in the sacrifice of Himself—in death—to forgive our sins and secure eternal life for us. His unselfishness was of infinite proportions, for He gave the immeasurable sacrifice. He came "to give His life a ransom for many" (Matthew 20:28). And why wouldn't He? Generosity is a part of His nature as God!

When you think about all that God the Father gave, the generosity of Jesus is no wonder. Throughout the Old Testament, from Genesis to Malachi, God is seen as a generous, loving, giving God. For example...

⟿ God gave life to Adam and Eve.

⟿ God gave safety and salvation to Noah and his family during the flood.

⟿ God gave manna to sustain the Israelites in the wilderness.

⟿ God gave the Promised Land to His chosen people.

⟿ God gave protection for His people while they served Him.

⟿ God gave David the promise of a future king, a Savior who would redeem man from his sin.

⟿ God gave His prophets visions of a coming Savior, His very own beloved Son.

⟿ God gave His only begotten Son.

As I just read and reflected on those instances of giving (especially the final one!), I had to ask myself, *What can I give...and what more can I give?* As children of the King, you and I have a privilege and a responsibility to continue our Father's example of giving—exceedingly abundantly above all that we ask or think. We have a reputation to uphold. Our character as Christians is involved. Do others see you as a giving person? As you read more of Jesus' examples of what it means to be charitable, make it a point to think and pray about what you can do to nurture a more generous spirit.

For Your Sake Jesus Became Poor

Our Jesus is a spectacular model of generosity and unselfishness. To begin the list, consider that He gave up His exalted place in heaven to become human. This does not mean He gave up His eternal powers; rather, it means He chose to live in obedience to the Father's will. "He became poor" when He became human because He sacrificed so much (2 Corinthians 8:9). In fact, He explained that "foxes have holes and birds of the air have nests, but the Son of Man has nowhere to lay His head" (Matthew 8:20). Yet His sacrifice—and generosity—in giving up everything, including the comforts of a home, was so that "you through His poverty might become rich" through receiving His free gift of salvation and eternal life (2 Corinthians 8:9).

Generosity, as defined by the life and character of Jesus, means sacrificial giving. To properly reflect Jesus' life, you may need to do what I did and turn the level of your generosity way up, all the way into the sacrificial range. Prayer and resolve is a good place to start...followed by action, of course.

The Widow Gave All She Had

Here's something to ponder: Generosity has nothing to do with how much you have, but everything to do with how much you give in proportion to how much you have. And Jesus showed us this truth through the actions of an amazing woman (you'll meet her again elsewhere in this book). Jesus pointed to an impoverished woman to illustrate the truth that God's definition of generosity is different than the world's definition. Jesus spotted her when He was with His disciples on the grounds of the temple and observing people in the act of placing their offerings into the temple treasury. Here's what happened:

> Now Jesus sat opposite the treasury and saw how the people put money into the treasury. And many who were rich put in much. Then one poor widow came and threw in two mites...So He called His disciples

> to Himself and said to them, "Assuredly, I say to you
> that this poor widow has put in more than all those
> who have given to the treasury; for they all put in
> out of their abundance, but she out of her poverty
> put in all that she had, her whole livelihood" (Mark
> 12:41-44).

Jesus explained that the widow gave more than all the others.
How was that possible? Because the others gave out of their material wealth at little personal cost and sacrifice. But the widow gave
out of her poverty. Proportionally she had given the most—all that
she had to live on! Such generous and sacrificial giving meant she
was completely trusting God to provide for all her needs.

Reflecting On Your Heart

> Jesus' message to your heart is this: Your generosity
> is not measured by the amount of your gift, but on
> the amount that is left over after you give. Obviously
> Jesus is not telling you to give everything you—and
> your family—have. But He *is* saying you're to give
> proportionally as God has blessed you and to trust
> Him to provide with what's left and to supply more
> if it's needed (2 Corinthians 9:7-8). There's no need
> to worry—the Lord is your shepherd; therefore, you
> will never lack what you truly need. He promises it
> in Psalm 23.

What can you do to follow in this lady's—and Jesus'—footsteps?
To start you off, pray about being more generous. If you have a
family, talk about this marvelous trait of generosity that Jesus possessed and looked for in others. What project can you or your family take on? This will speak volumes to your kids, and it will water
and nurture this stellar quality of generosity in their hearts too.

Where Your Treasure Is, There Your Heart Will Be

This book is about reflecting Jesus' heart. Like all of the character traits in Jesus, generosity is a matter of the heart. The Pharisees, a sect of religious leaders in Jesus' day, made a great show of giving to the needy, both in the synagogues and on the streets. They thought this proved how righteous and spiritual they were.

However, Jesus taught just the opposite regarding generosity. He said giving should be done in secret. He instructed us to "take heed that you do not do your charitable deeds before men, to be seen by them." Instead, you are to not even "let your left hand know what your right hand is doing." Why? "That your charitable deed may be in secret; and your Father who sees in secret will Himself reward you openly" (Matthew 6:1,2-4).

Giving God's way demonstrates true righteousness before God, not in front of others, And the result? God in turn rewards the giver. In other words, you cannot look for your blessings and rewards from both man and God.

Reflecting On Your Heart

Giving is a matter between you and God and not you and another person or cause, no matter how important it is. It's a matter of the heart. Giving is to be an act of worship. Just as you prepare yourself for worship and ministry, you are to prepare yourself for acts of generosity (2 Corinthians 9:7). Where's your heart? A guiding truth teaches that "where your treasure is, there your heart will be also" (Matthew 6:21).

Do Good to Those Who Hate You

It's natural to enjoy being generous to our friends and those who are generous to us or even to those who are in dire need. But our attitudes change when it comes to giving to those who hurt us. Our human nature generally wants retaliation when we're harmed. But Jesus took the concept of love and generosity to a whole new level. He taught that generosity also applies to our enemies. We are to treat others—and specifically our enemies—differently. Instead of seeking revenge by retaliating or withholding, we are to "give to him who asks you, and from him who wants to borrow from you do not turn away" (Matthew 5:42), even if that person is an enemy.

Jesus never made an idle statement. When He was dying on the cross He did not ask for retaliation or justice. Instead, He asked that His enemies—those who condemned and killed Him—be forgiven. He prayed, "Father, forgive them, for they do not know what they do" (Luke 23:34).

My favorite teaching on how to treat my enemies gives us Jesus' three-step, surefire way of loving our enemies. He said to "love your enemies." How is that accomplished? "Bless those who curse you, do good to those who hate you, and pray for those who spitefully use you and persecute you" (Matthew 5:44). So get your heart, mouth, and spirit ready to love! You'll need them to bless, do good, and pray for your enemies.

Test your own generous nature by seeking out someone who's been mean to you. Pick out someone who's slandered you or hurt you or your family in some way. Ask God to give you strength to model Jesus' love and goodness. Then bless her verbally by speaking positively about her. Give her something that's personal and of value to you, such as forgiveness from your heart. And pray for her, for her success, for her relationship with God. When you do these things from a heart of love, God is honored, and you reflect the generous heart of Jesus.

Give to the Poor, and Follow Jesus

Do you realize that the level of a person's generosity indicates the level of his or her commitment to Christ? In Matthew 19:16-22, Jesus met two men toward the end of His three-plus years of ministry. The first, a rich young ruler, indicated he wanted to follow Jesus and asked what he needed to do to make this happen. Jesus' answer? "Sell what you have and give to the poor, and you will have treasure in heaven; and come, follow Me" (verse 21). The encounter ends with the young man walking away in disappointment because "he had great possessions" (verse 22).

The second man Jesus met was Zacchaeus (see Luke 19:1-9). Like the rich young ruler, Zacchaeus wanted to see Jesus. When Jesus acknowledged Zacchaeus and invited Himself to his house for dinner, Zacchaeus declared, "Look, Lord, I give half of my goods to the poor; and if I have taken anything from anyone by false accusation, I restore fourfold" (verse 8). He voluntarily offered to give half of his possessions and wealth to the poor. And, if he had cheated anybody out of anything, he would pay it back 100 percent...times four!

Both men were seeking and wanted to follow Jesus. In response, Jesus offered the first man a quick test to measure the true nature of his heart. The result? He was not willing to part with his money. The second man, however, responded with an overabundance of generosity without even being asked, revealing a true commitment to follow Jesus.

We both know generosity is not necessarily an indicator of a relationship with Jesus. There are many charitable people in the world who are not Christians. But those who have a heart for Jesus and sincerely desire to follow Him are generous—like Him! He instructed us to "seek first the kingdom of God and His righteousness, and all these things shall be added to you" (Matthew 6:33). Unfortunately we tend to get this backward. We seek "things" first and add Jesus on as an afterthought.

Reflecting On Your Heart

If you're feeling the need for a priority makeover, a look at your checkbook or your monthly credit card statement will shout out what you are seeking— things, or the things of God. Take a peek. It's a little like taking your temperature. See what it reveals about the level of your commitment to things versus the things Jesus values. What does it disclose about your heart-attitude toward money and possessions and generosity?

Lay Up for Yourselves Treasure in Heaven

When Jesus preached His famous Sermon on the Mount, He spoke to His disciples and the assembled crowd, contrasting kingdom living with worldly living. The world, He pointed out, is obsessed with selfishly amassing earthly wealth. But to His followers Jesus taught quite a different philosophy, which still stands today. He said, "Do not lay up for yourselves treasures on earth, where moth and rust destroy and where thieves break in and steal; but lay up for yourselves treasures in heaven...For where your treasure is, there your heart will be also" (Matthew 6:19-21).

Jesus contrasted heavenly values with earthly ones. He explained that our first loyalty should be to those things that don't corrode and can't be stolen. How can we be sure that our investments are safe? Jesus said we should invest in the things of God. What's given to God and to His purposes is an investment in heaven, in things that matter on an everlasting forever scale. It doesn't matter what happens to the stock market, or the housing market, or at the grocery market. Anything and everything invested with God will have eternal value! That's the ultimate investment. Your generosity is a cure for selfishness. It's the ultimate hedge against the temptation to selfishly hoard money that helps no one, can be stolen, or can disappear during the down periods on the stock and real estate markets.

Jesus' final statement in verse 21—"Where your treasure is, there your heart will be also"—is a key principle to remember and memorize. It points out that whatever occupies our thoughts and time is where our affections will be.

Maybe as these teachings from Jesus are echoing in your heart and mind, it's a good time to again evaluate how much you love the treasures of this world—your money, your house, your car, your possessions. Exactly where is your treasure? How tightly are you holding on to your riches? Can you live without them? If you can't let loose of some of those treasures, you don't own them—they own you. Ask God for His help. Ask Him to expose any personal areas of worldliness. What can you give away or put to use that would aid someone else and at the same time demonstrate to yourself and to God that your heart—and therefore your treasure—is in heaven?

Reflecting the Heart of Jesus

Can you imagine having everything and yet being willing to give it all up? Well, that's the model that's presented to you and me in the life of Jesus. If you want to reflect the heart of Jesus and mirror His character, then generosity is a must. It's true that no one can out-give God, and if you are a child of God, you should desire to give and give generously to others. As Jesus told His disciples, "Freely you have received, freely give" (Matthew 10:8).

Think of all the blessings God has showered upon you. Salvation. The forgiveness of sin. The promise of eternal life. Like Jesus instructed the Twelve, you should freely give—not only your possessions and money, but your time, your help, your ministry, your mercy, and most of all, your love.

～ A Prayer to Pray ～

Lord Jesus, thank You that You gave the ultimate gift when You sacrificed Yourself to pay for my sins. May I too become a generous giver with no motives and no worries, only a desire to follow You and bless others. Amen.

Gentle

When cigarette companies were still allowed to advertise on television, one company put out an appeal to women using the slogan "You've come a long way, baby!" With these words the company was suggesting that women were ready to "get with it" and take up the habit of smoking. Well, research now shows what could result physically to the women who succumbed to those ads. Just read the surgeon general's cancer warning printed on every package of cigarettes!

Unfortunately, women also embraced the slogan "You've come a long way, baby!" for other areas of life. Some have taken on an attitude of defiance and belligerence. And others have become more assertive, aggressive, outspoken, self-reliant, and self-centered. As we live in a world that encourages self-absorption and prideful arrogance, we must be oh-so-careful not to give up the gentleness that God desires in us. We have to be on guard not to trade in an incredibly beautiful gentle spirit for a mean toughness that's anything but beautiful.

Jesus Shows Us the Way

Before we look to Jesus, let's define *gentleness*. To begin, it has nothing to do with being a woman. It is a quality all Christians are to exhibit. And it's a fruit of the Spirit, showing evidence that a believer is walking in sync with God. The world views gentleness as a sign of weakness. But in reality, gentleness is like a two-sided coin. One side conveys the idea of meekness, humility, or lowliness. It possesses patience, a wait-and-see attitude as it quietly and calmly looks at the facts of each situation in a coolheaded manner. Yet when we turn the coin over, we discover that gentleness requires the firmness of self-mastery, of strength under control. It demands steel-like self-discipline. It has the power to endure provocation and suffering. Gentleness, in essence, "takes it," whatever the "it" might be. It is the powerful opposite of self-reliant arrogance or brazen assertiveness.

As you approach another quality today, it's not surprising that Jesus is the ultimate example of gentleness. Take a look at His gentleness now.

Take My Yoke upon You

During His years of ministry, Jesus saw firsthand the religious burdens the Jewish leaders were placing upon the people. Moved by their condition, Jesus offered to relieve the people of these burdens if they would come to Him. In contrast to the harsh demands of a religious works system, Jesus described Himself as gentle. He invited the downhearted masses to "come to Me, all you who labor and are heavy laden, and I will give you rest. Take My yoke upon you and learn from Me, for I am gentle and lowly in heart, and you will find rest for your souls. For My yoke is easy and My burden is light" (Matthew 11:28-30).

Reflecting On Your Heart

Are you weary of shouldering the heavy burdens that have resulted from trying to do things on your own, or from following after the will and advice of others? Has your self-reliance yielded less-than-satisfying results? Are your bold, assertive methods of handling life and people backfiring? Whatever the burden, Jesus offers relief as you exchange your methods of managing life for the ease that comes from yoking yourself with Jesus. When yoked together with Him, you will enjoy the peace of mind dependence on Him brings to your heart. When you make this exchange and join up with Jesus, you will find rest for your soul and from life's burdens. To walk through life with Jesus and to love and serve Him is no burden, for He is gentle and His load is light.

Your King Is Coming

Jesus spent three years humbly ministering to the people in and around Palestine. In time the day finally arrived when He began moving toward Jerusalem and His death. As the King of kings and Lord of lords rode into Jerusalem, Matthew wrote (quoting from an Old Testament prophecy), "Behold your King is coming to you, gentle, and mounted on a donkey" (Matthew 21:5 NASB).

Think about it. Christ appeared in Jerusalem, the city of Zion, not in His glory, but in meekness. Not in His majesty, but in mercy. Not to conquer, but to bring about salvation for sinners. Gentleness and outward poverty were the identifying qualities of Zion's king and characterized His ministry. Jesus could have asserted Himself at any point. He could have demanded respect, allegiance, and royal treatment. He could have thundered into town like a king and triumphant conqueror in a gold-covered chariot with divisions of soldiers marching behind it. Yet Jesus chose to make His entrance into Jerusalem in meekness, on a borrowed donkey.

Reflecting On Your Heart

Unlike the crowd that greeted Jesus in Jerusalem, who saw Him as some sort of folk hero rather than the Messiah and Savior, you know the real Jesus. And this should prompt you to greater levels of passionate praise and worship. If you have a genuine relationship with Jesus, make sure your times of worship, whether private or public, properly and respectfully communicate your love and adoration for your Savior. Look forward to time in His presence. Be faithful in showing up at church and to your quiet times.

Welcome Him to your time of worship. Give Him the red carpet treatment with praise and adoration and celebration. Joyfully receive Him and celebrate your King.

Others Show Us the Way

He Fell on His Face

Moses, the servant of God—When you think of Moses, you might not immediately think of gentleness. That's because Moses was a leader's leader and in charge of more than two million people. This mass of humanity was constantly murmuring, grumbling, and complaining. Even though they had a miserable suppressed life as slaves in Egypt, they decided that being in Egypt was far better than following Moses and wandering around the desert. In spite of their rebellious attitude, Moses led them to the borders of the Promised Land. How did he accomplish this almost impossible task while being confronted, accused, slandered, and put down by an obstinate group for 40 years? On four separate occasions when his leadership was questioned, we learn that...

- Moses "cried out to the LORD" (Exodus 15:25);

- "Moses cried out to the LORD" (Exodus 17:1-4);

- "Moses and Aaron fell on their faces" (Numbers 14:5);

- "when Moses heard [of the utter rebellion against him], he fell on his face" (Numbers 16:3-4).

Whether the people complained, rebelled, or unjustly accused him, Moses didn't argue, struggle, or try to defend himself. No, he exhibited gentleness while under attack. He patiently endured. He silently bore their offences and openly cried out to the Lord. Moses "took it" ...and then he took it to God, appealing to God and waiting on Him to come to his rescue.

In Moses we see the grace of gentleness lived out. He took the accusations and criticism and did nothing, trusting everything into God's care. When God evaluated Moses' heart, He testified "the man Moses was very meek, above all the men who were upon the face of the earth" (Numbers 12:3 KJV). We have one giant lesson to learn from Moses: When wronged and misunderstood, submit yourself in gentle humility into the mighty hands of God "that He may exalt you in due time" (1 Peter 5:6).

Let It Be to Me According to Your Word

Mary, the maidservant of the Lord—In Mary, the mother of Jesus, we find another inspiring example of gentleness. When Mary was told by the angel Gabriel that she would have a baby who would be the Messiah, what was her response? She submitted to God's plan, saying, "Behold the maidservant of the Lord! Let it be to me according to your word" (Luke 1:38). For the next 33 years while Jesus walked on earth, Mary silently endured the shadow of doubt her obedience to God's will cast across her reputation (John 8:41). It wasn't until the resurrection of the Son of God that the cloud hanging over Mary's life was lifted.

Gentleness and Your Walk with Jesus

Are you grasping how important gentleness is? It's an essential element in your walk with Christ. As you take a further look at what the Bible says about gentleness, I think you'll agree that when you exhibit gentleness, or meekness, you reflect Jesus.

Gentleness is a key to abundant living—"Blessed are the meek, for they shall inherit the earth" (Matthew 5:5).

Gentleness can bring peace instead of strife—Note these contrasts: "A soft [gentle] answer turns away wrath, but a harsh word stirs up anger" (Proverbs. 15:1), and "A hot-tempered man stirs up dissension, but a patient man calms a quarrel" (verse 18 NIV). A gentle attitude will defuse a situation and make it easier to settle a matter peacefully.

Gentleness is considerate of others even when confrontation is necessary—"If anyone is caught in any trespass, you who are spiritual, restore such a one in a spirit of gentleness" (Galatians 6:1 NASB). Gentleness seeks restoration rather than lashing out at a sinning brother or sister in Christ.

Gentleness is a reflection of love—"With all lowliness and gentleness, with longsuffering, [bear] with one another in love" (Ephesians 4:2). A gentle spirit goes a long way in preserving unity in the body of Christ.

Gentleness is one of the defining characteristics of a Christian—"As the elect of God, holy and beloved, put on tender mercies, kindness, humility, meekness, longsuffering" (Colossians 3:12-13).

Gentleness is patient with those who oppose—"A servant of the Lord must not quarrel but be gentle to all, able to teach, patient, in humility correcting those who are in opposition" (2 Timothy 2:24-25).

Gentleness is confident yet respectful—"Be ready to give a defense to everyone who asks you a reason for the hope that is in you, with meekness and fear" (1 Peter 3:15).

Gentleness marks a person who is submissive to God's Word—"Lay aside all filthiness and overflow of wickedness, and receive with meekness the implanted word" (James 1:21).

Gentleness in a woman is precious to God—"Do not let your adornment be merely outward...rather let it be the hidden person of the heart, with the incorruptible beauty of a gentle and quiet spirit, which is very precious in the sight of God" (1 Peter 3:3-4).

Gentleness is like an ornament you wear. It's not something that's seen like clothes, but an ornament of the heart. When worn, gentleness doesn't cause any disturbances. And when put together with "a quiet spirit," it means that God's woman doesn't create disturbances, and she doesn't react to the disturbances created by others.

Reflecting the Heart of Jesus

No matter how society or those around you regard gentleness, it is an exquisite, powerful, and lofty Christlike attitude. To reflect this precious-in-the-sight-of-God quality, first desire it with all your heart. Then take every opportunity to bear mistreatment or misunderstanding with tranquility. Like Moses, fall on your face before God and wait for His action on your behalf. In prayer, seek His wisdom for your every move. Trust in the Lord to protect you and guide you, to empower you with His grace to respond to trials with Jesus' gentleness.

⌐ A Prayer to Pray ⌐

Lord Jesus, by Your grace may I accept what happens in my life as part of Your purpose. May I gently submit to each situation without complaining. May I refrain from trying to manipulate my way out of problems. May I remember to trust You and count on Your love. Thank You that each difficulty handled with gentleness makes me more like You. Amen.

Good

They're good people" is not something you often hear said about many people, is it? Goodness, like most of the qualities we're admiring in our dear Savior's life, seems to be less important in our society as we tend to center on taking care of Number One, ourselves. Sadly, the news is made up mostly of stories about what the Bible describes as "deeds of the flesh" (see Galatians 5:19-21 NASB). Maybe that's why *The Weather Channel* is often my first choice in TV viewing!

But all is not lost. There are still good people in this world who are busily going about doing good. If you're reading this book about Christlike character, you're probably interested in goodness. Like the other qualities we're admiring throughout this book, goodness is contagious. Each and every good thing you or I do sets an example for others. Each good deed is like a stone dropped in a still pond. The ripples created by that one stone spread outward across the entire body of water. So drop your goodness into the pool of life and watch the ripples spread!

God Shows Us the Way

God is a great God. But if greatness was His only attribute, He could conceivably be an immoral or amoral being, exercising His power and knowledge in an impulsive and cruel fashion. There have been many kings and rulers down through the centuries who have been great, but were also vicious and vengeful. Yet when we understand that God is also a good God, we add morality to His being. Whatever God does can only be good because that's who He is. It's His very nature.

When God's servant Moses wanted to know more about the God he was to represent to the people, Moses asked God, "Please, show me Your glory" (Exodus 33:18). Before God passed before Moses, He made this statement: "I will make all My goodness pass before you" (verse 19). Then as God passed before Moses, He proclaimed, "The LORD, the LORD God, merciful and gracious, longsuffering, and abounding in goodness and truth" (34:6).

God abounds in goodness. His every activity is only good. Therefore, whatever He allows to happen in our lives can only be classified as good. As God, He could not allow it to be otherwise. The apostle Paul understood this concept of God's goodness when he wrote that believers in God's Son can "know that all things work together for good to those who love God, to those who are the called according to His purpose" (Romans 8:28).

Jesus Shows Us the Way

Because God the Father is morally good and can only do good, we know that His only Son, Jesus, is also good and can only do good. Hear now as He teaches about goodness.

Good Teacher, What Good Thing Shall I Do?

We've come across this young man before in his encounter with Jesus. But this time notice how the rich young ruler addressed and referred to Jesus. When he approached the Lord, he said, "Good Teacher, what good thing shall I do that I may have eternal life?" (Matthew 19:16). The young ruler wanted to know what good work would demonstrate that he was righteous and would therefore qualify him for eternal life. Jesus replied, "Why do you call Me good? No one is good but One, that is, God" (verse 17).

Perhaps Jesus then waited for a response from the ruler to see if he would affirm his belief that Jesus was God. Unfortunately, the young man was still looking to his own "good works" to get him into heaven and missed out on the true source of goodness—salvation through Jesus Christ.

Lord, Do You Want Us to Command Fire?

As we step into this scene, realize that, unlike our fleshly nature, God is not cruel or vengeful. And, like His Father, Jesus is only capable of good. In Him there is no evil. Jesus' goodness and man's vileness are illustrated in Luke 9:51-56. Here's what happened: Jesus and His disciples were steadily moving toward Jerusalem, where the cross and death awaited Jesus. They were on a march because Jesus had "steadfastly set His face to go to Jerusalem" (verse 51). Jesus sent some of His disciples ahead to make arrangements for Him in a Samaritan village. However, because the party (being Jews) was traveling toward Jerusalem, the town's people (who were not Jews) refused them any form of hospitality.

Well, this snubbing of the Lord was taken seriously by the disciples! That was especially true about James and his brother John. We've met them before in this same situation, but here we see them live out the name Jesus gave these two brothers—"Boanerges, that is, 'Sons of Thunder'" (Mark 3:17). The ill treatment of Jesus was such a major issue for them that they reacted and asked Jesus, "Lord, do You want us to command fire to come down from heaven and consume them?" (Luke 9:54).

What was Jesus' response? "He turned and rebuked them, and said, 'You do not know what manner of spirit you are of. For the Son of Man did not come to destroy men's lives but to save them'" (verses 55-56).

In Jesus we see goodness as opposed to the disciples' aggressive and judgmental spirit. Jesus demonstrated what goodness is all about—not destroying others, no matter how badly they treat you, but helping and loving them instead. Think about it: Jesus was the one who had been rejected, not the disciples. Furthermore, He had the power to avenge Himself. He indeed could have called down fire! But He chose not to retaliate. He demonstrated goodness instead. He wanted what was best for this Samaritan village, no matter how they treated Him or His disciples.

And here's another insight: Jesus' goodness kept Him moving

toward Jerusalem to die for these very same people, the Samaritans, and all those like them, who had rejected Him.

Reflecting On Your Heart

Have you ever taken—or thought of taking—the same approach as these proud disciples? When you're rejected, rebuffed, or ignored, do you take it personally and let your feelings get hurt? Do you lash out? Do you imagine or come up with a few creative ways to get back at those who disrespect or disregard or harm you? It's so natural and easy to respond in such ways, isn't it? To take "an eye for an eye" approach? But what should you do instead when you're wronged or ill-treated? One way you can respond is to follow Jesus' example and do nothing. Then, while you are doing nothing, you can pray. Take time to reflect on God's way of treating those who cause anguish. God's brand of goodness will not retaliate with evil, but will instead find ways to show kindness. Just think: Every mean or cruel act done against you is an opportunity for you to reflect Jesus, to magnificently display a Godlike response and dispense God's goodness.

When You Do a Charitable Deed

Don't you feel good when you do something meaningful? When you're involved in doing something good, it just seems to make your day a little brighter, doesn't it? Normally we don't—and shouldn't—want or desire recognition for doing a good deed. But occasionally it is genuinely refreshing when you are acknowledged for some act of kindness. After all, encouraging words and a pat on the back provide fuel for meeting the next need. But read on for a word of caution from Jesus.

The Jewish leaders in Jesus' day did many good works. There was just one problem: Most of their good works were done with a desire to be noticed and praised by others. They wanted to hear how great they were and how outstanding their deeds were. But in seeking the reward of praise from others they missed out on the real reward, the one that comes from God alone. Jesus called this kind of person a hypocrite and told His followers—and you and me—how to perform good deeds. His advice? "When you do a charitable deed, do not let your left hand know what your right hand is doing, that your charitable deed may be in secret; and your Father who sees in secret will Himself reward you openly" (Matthew 6:3-4). And that's a promise!

Reflecting On Your Heart

Doing good is a good thing to strive for. When you do a good deed, praise God for the great feelings it brings to your heart. If you receive the praise of others, see that as an added blessing. But keep your focus on the people you're helping, not on what you might gain for yourself. Set your heart on the praise that's waiting in heaven. This is the eternal reward you are waiting for: "Well done, good and faithful servant" (Matthew 25:23).

Goodness and Good Works

When we dedicate ourselves to helping others to live better, Jesus' goodness is activated. Then when we see an opportunity to help others, His goodness goes into action. This is the beautiful way God wants us to live. He calls us as His women to goodness and good works.

∽ Older women are to be models of goodness in their behavior, speech, and habits—being "reverent in behavior, not slanderers, not given to much wine" (Titus 2:3).

∽ Older women are to be "teachers of good things" (verse 3).

~ Younger women are to learn about goodness so they are able "to love their husbands, to love their children, to be discreet, chaste, homemakers, good, obedient to their own husbands" (verses 4-5).

~ Women are to be devoted to goodness and good works, "well reported for good works: if she has brought up children, if she has lodged strangers, if she has washed the saints' feet, if she has relieved the afflicted, if she has diligently followed every good work" (1 Timothy 5:10).

~ Women are to put on the garments of goodness. They are exhorted to "adorn themselves...with good works" (1 Timothy 2:9-10).

Work at Doing What Is Good

Beyond God's desire for goodness in our roles as women, wives, and moms, God calls all His children to a life of goodness and a ministry of doing good.

~ Work at doing what is good—God will reward "glory, honor, and peace to everyone who works what is good" (Romans 2:10).

~ Prove what is good—"Do not be conformed to this world, but be transformed by the renewing of your mind, that you may prove what is that good and acceptable and perfect will of God" (Romans 12:2).

~ Hold fast to what is good—"Abhor what is evil. Cling to what is good" (Romans 12:9).

~ Overcome evil with good—"Do not be overcome by evil, but overcome evil with good" (Romans 12:21).

~ Strive to do what is good—"Rulers are not a terror to good works, but to evil. Do you want to be unafraid of the authority? Do what is good, and you will have praise from the same" (Romans 13:3).

∼ Follow after what is good—"See that no one renders evil for evil to anyone, but always pursue what is good both for yourselves and for all" (1 Thessalonians 5:15).

∼ Be zealous for what is good—"Who is he who will harm you if you become followers of what is good?" (1 Peter 3:13).

Reflecting the Heart of Jesus

"Jesus...went about doing good" (Acts 10:38). These five words inspire me every single day. I quote them to myself, fix them in my heart, and let them guide my deeds for one more day. Jesus accomplished so very much during His lifetime, and it all came from His goodness!

The Bible says that Jesus is the key to your goodness (Romans 3:12). This means that the only way to reflect the goodness of Jesus is to get close to Him, and let His character rub off on you. Stay near to Him until you don't know any other way to walk and live except by going about doing what is good!

So pray daily for Christ's goodness to flow through you to others. Be on the lookout for opportunities to show His goodness in deeds of kindness. And once you spot an opportunity or think of something that would make someone else's days go better, don't stop! Put your observations and kind thoughts into action. Do everything Jesus brings to your mind to better the lives of others, to help lighten the load of the burdens they bear, to encourage faint hearts and lift their sorrows. Reflect the heart of Jesus by acting in goodness.

∼ A Prayer to Pray ∼

Good Teacher, fill my mind with kind thoughts toward all people. Help me to be less self-absorbed so I don't fail to notice those who are downcast or in need. Give me the grace to pour forth the riches of Your goodness as freely as You did. Amen.

Gracious

I grew up in Oklahoma, where the elements of Southern living and hospitality created a way of life. Most of the mothers in my circle of girlfriends were socially gracious in appearance and behavior. Their dinner parties and gatherings were pictures of elegance. And believe me, my friends and I were carefully taught and groomed by our moms to be gracious and practice good etiquette, especially when we were in public. Our graciousness was learned, appropriate behavior. And because it was externally induced by our parents, it could be turned on and off like a light fixture. Graciousness became an act that we put on when it was required, expected, or beneficial in getting something we wanted.

Like me, anyone can be trained to be gracious. But when I became a Christian, I realized that true biblical graciousness is an attitude of the heart. It's not something we want to turn on and off, but something we want to live by, something we want prominently embedded at the core of our being.

Jesus Shows Us the Way

Jesus. Just say His name and the word *grace* snaps into my mind, and maybe yours too. Jesus was gracious, giving, generous, and extended the marvelous grace of His salvation to sinners. As we arrive at this "marvelous" virtue on our walk through Jesus' life and character qualities, it's no surprise that we find it fully and perfectly lived out by our Lord.

A gracious person, in our culture, is someone who shows respect, honor, and kindness to others. In Bible times a gracious person was usually a person of superior position and power who showed favor and mercy to someone in an inferior position with little or no power. For example, in the Old Testament, the Egyptian officer Potiphar dealt graciously with his slave, Joseph; the destitute Ruth found favor in the eyes of Boaz; and the young Jewish girl Esther was treated respectfully by King Ahasuerus.[4] And God, who was gracious toward mankind, describes Himself as "the LORD God, merciful and gracious" (Exodus 34:6).

In the New Testament, God's grace is a manifestation of His love. Grace is the means God uses to deal with His people, not on the basis of their merit, worthiness, or behavior, but because of His goodness and generosity. Grace describes all that God has done for you and me through Christ.[5]

As we look at Jesus, we see that the Son of God, the very image of the Father, possessed graciousness and conducted Himself in gracious behavior at all times while He was on earth. The following scenarios from His life point out His gracious way with people. You'll see a few folks you've met before in this book, but this time we are examining the grace of our Lord to people like you and me.

All Marveled at the Gracious Words

Jesus was a teacher, and a teacher must teach. The Bible reports that on one occasion, "as His custom was, He went into the synagogue on the Sabbath day, and stood up to read" (Luke 4:16). After reading from the Scriptures, Jesus sat down to teach His listeners what the passage meant. What was the response of those who heard Him that day? "All bore witness to Him, and marveled at the gracious words which proceeded out of His mouth" (verse 22).

Jesus' ministry was characterized by grace. His words were both kind and wise. He didn't practice flattery or use exaggeration. And His words weren't merely appealing. Instead, He spoke truth with authority because He spoke words from God.

As a Christian woman who represents Jesus to others, the source of your speech is your own heart.
So, if you walk by God's Spirit, His love, patience,
goodness, kindness, gentleness, and self-control are
present. Then your choice of words will make these
Godlike qualities evident. One key way to be gracious in speech is to follow Paul's guideline: "Let no
corrupt word proceed out of your mouth, but what
is good for necessary edification, that it may impart
grace to the hearers" (Ephesians 4:29).

You Are Troubled About Many Things

Poor Martha! As you read Luke 10:38-42, you'll see that Martha
definitely lost control. According to this brief sketch, she graciously
opened her home to Jesus and His 12 disciples. Serving and host-
ing this large group was a lot of work! Initially her sister, Mary,
helped her. But when Jesus began teaching, Mary planted herself
at His feet and was all ears. Well, Martha lost her cool...and her
manners. She burst into the room, interrupted the Teacher, slandered Mary, and lit into the Lord, accusing Him of not caring.

Wow! Aren't you embarrassed for Martha? How did Jesus respond to her impatience and frustration, her condemning attitude
and speech? Jesus answered, "Martha, Martha, you are worried and
troubled about many things. But one thing is needed, and Mary
has chosen that good part, which will not be taken away from
her" (Luke 10:41-42).

Jesus could have dealt harshly with Martha. She certainly deserved rebuke. But that wasn't Jesus' style. He graciously spoke
her name twice, acknowledged her concerns about preparing the
meal and wanting Him and the disciples to feel welcomed and
cared for. But He also let her know she had missed the point of
her giving and service. Jesus wanted to gently show her the real
priorities, the "good part" she was missing out on—knowing, hearing, and worshiping Him.

Reflecting On Your Heart

What is your patience level when someone misses the point of your communication or misses out on picking up on your need...or misses the big picture? How gracious are you with these people? And what about your children, when they don't seem to listen to you and your instructions? You can get mad or upset. You can rant and rave. You can let others have it with your words. And you can rationalize your actions all you want. But you are to handle these everyday situations in a Christlike manner—with graciousness. Show patience and kindness to those who aren't where you are, or haven't quite grasped the bigger picture. Follow Jesus' example and Paul's exhortation "to speak evil of no one, to be peaceable, gentle, showing all humility to all men" (Titus 3:2). Be gracious.

What Do You Want Me to Do for You?

Compassion and mercy are similar attitudes to graciousness. A gracious person is usually a compassionate person, and a compassionate person is usually gracious. Jesus showed these two attitudes in tandem as He made His way through Jericho on His way to Jerusalem and His triumphal entry into the city. As He was leaving Jericho, two blind beggars called out to Him as He walked by.

Then the multitude warned them that they should be quiet; but they cried out all the more, saying, "Have mercy on us, O Lord, Son of David!" So Jesus stood still and called them, and said, "What do you want Me to do for you?" They said to Him, "Lord, that our eyes may be opened." So Jesus had compassion and touched their eyes. And immediately their eyes received sight, and they followed Him (Matthew 20:31-34).

Jesus healed numerous blind people during His three-year ministry. The blind and the sick never stopped coming to Him, and there is no record of His refusing any of them who approached Him for help. But note Jesus' graciousness in this example. These needy men were told by the crowd to stay quiet, to quit calling to Jesus as He passed by. But Jesus heard them, stopped, asked them what they wanted from Him, and then complied with their request. Unlike the people, He treated them graciously and with respect. He was filled with mercy and compassion, He graciously extended the grace of God by restoring their sight.

Reflecting On Your Heart

Biblical grace is defined as God's unmerited favor offered to those who don't deserve it. Jesus asked these men, "What do you want Me to do for you?" Do you think of yourself as a gracious person? Hopefully you are! If so, you are walking among God's creation showing forth His grace mixed in with His compassion and mercy. You are reflecting the great and gracious heart of Jesus. If you need a grace prod, put at the top of your daily prayer list a reminder to ask God to help you remember to be gracious. Then, when you are out and about, you can ask others, "How can I help you today?" Or you can ask yourself as you encounter others, "What favor can I extend to this person I'm with right now?" Looking at others through eyes of love will result in gracious words and works.

I Have Prayed for You

Peter was always seen as the leader of the disciples. He is listed first each time the disciples are named in Scripture. He was the spokesman for the group. Jesus even referred to Peter as a "rock" (Matthew 16:17-18). It's no wonder Jesus was counting on Peter to serve as the leader of the group after He ascended into heaven.

The night before His betrayal, Jesus knew exactly what was going to happen when He and the Twelve left the upper room. He knew Peter would deny Him. In fact, Jesus described to Peter what was going to happen. He looked at Peter and graciously said, "Simon, Simon! Indeed, Satan has asked for you, that he may sift you as wheat" (Luke 22:31). This sounds similar to Jesus' encouraging remarks to Martha. But then Jesus added, "I have prayed for you, that your faith should not fail; and when you have returned to Me, strengthen your brethren" (verse 32).

Jesus never gave up on Peter, no matter how brash or foolish he acted. The all-knowing Jesus knew everything about Peter's shortcomings. Instead of washing His hands and discarding a faulty disciple, Jesus still believed in Peter and had already prayed that Peter would bounce back from his bout with failure.

Reflecting On Your Heart

It's always good to have people you can depend on. They're there when you need them. And the greater your dependence upon them, the greater your expectations of them. You count on these people to come through for you. But at times they fail. How do you act (or react!) when someone lets you down? Don't follow the natural responses of venting anger or berating and humiliating the poor offender. Follow Jesus' example and try to graciously understand what might have happened to cause this person to let you down. Like Jesus who saw the potential in Peter, look beyond the failure and recall the reasons you've depended on this person in the past. And, like Jesus, seek to graciously restore the person to usefulness.

The Proverbs 31 Woman
Shows Us the Way

The writer of a passage at the end of the book of Proverbs spoke of a gracious and godly woman often referred to as the Proverbs 31 woman. He described her with the query, "Who can find a virtuous woman? For her price is far above rubies" (Proverbs 31:10 KJV). God's excellent woman, whether she is married or single, has graciousness stamped on every part of her nature.

What do people see when this gracious woman walks into a room? What is her demeanor? "Strength and honor are her clothing" (verse 25).

What is her attitude toward others, especially the less fortunate? "She extends her hand to the poor, yes, she reaches out her hands to the needy" (verse 20).

What is the manner of her speech? "She opens her mouth with wisdom, and on her tongue is the law of kindness" (verse 26).

What is the key to her character? "Charm is deceitful and beauty is passing, but a woman who fears the LORD, she shall be praised" (verse 30).

Reflecting the Heart of Jesus

Jesus was perfectly gracious. Because of His love, He was warm, courteous, and kind. He didn't merely turn on graciousness when needed and then just as easily turn it off. No, Jesus was gracious in nature. He was gracious all the time. That's how you can reflect the heart of Jesus. You reflect Him when your heart is filled with His love, and your lips overflow with gracious words. When you extend the gracious spirit of the Lord, people will feel welcome and cared for when they're in your presence. And best of all, your graciousness will draw people to Jesus as they are drawn to His reflection in you.

～ A Prayer to Pray ～

Gracious Lord, thank You for the wonderful, matchless grace You show toward me. Your love is completely undeserved and therefore full of grace. Please help me love You even more. And please enable me to extend Your loving, genuine grace to others. Amen.

Humble

I often teach from the book of Esther and, like many women, I absolutely love the tale of this beautiful, heroic queen of the Old Testament. She had no parents, and was taken from her home in a roundup of the best-looking young women throughout the Persian Empire. There she was kept in the king's harem to be groomed and presented to him as a candidate for the king's next wife and queen, if he so chose.

One resource I found while preparing for my classes is an invaluable volume on Esther's life written by Charles R. Swindoll. In his commentary on the book of Esther, he writes this about humility:

> We're never once commanded by God to "look" humble. Humility is an attitude. It is an attitude of the heart. An attitude of the mind. It is knowing your proper place…It is knowing your role and fulfilling it for God's glory and praise.[6]

Jesus Shows Us the Way

Think about this for a minute. Jesus was God-in-flesh, all-powerful and omnipotent. This means He possessed the creative strength and almighty power that God the Father possesses. He could perform miracles—and did. And one day in the future, He will use His incomparable power to rule as King of kings and Lord of lords.

And yet it is this same Jesus who stands for all time as the ultimate example of humility. Jesus' path of humble service from birth to the cross is the pattern we're to follow and a quality we're to reflect. Scripture tells us to...

> let this mind be in you which was also in Christ Jesus, who, being in the form of God...made Himself of no reputation, taking the form of a bondservant, and coming in the likeness of men. And being found in appearance as a man, He humbled Himself and became obedient to the point of death, even the death of the cross (Philippians 2:5-8).

After humbling Himself to become a man, Jesus further lowered Himself by refusing to demand certain human rights while on earth. Instead He subjected Himself to persecution and suffering at the hands of cruel unbelievers. Beyond the persecution, Jesus went to the ultimate expression in His humiliation by dying as a criminal, obediently following the Father's plan for Him.

As we begin today to look at Jesus' humility, consider how this godly attitude should become an important quality in your everyday life. As I read in my research, "If we say we follow Christ, we must also say we want to live as he lived."[7] I know from experience that humility goes against everything in our human nature. We are naturally selfish and self-centered people who think first and foremost about ourselves. But, as the scripture above says, you and I are to "let this mind be in you which was also in Christ Jesus." Here are a few "how tos" for nurturing humility. Some are positive, and some negative. All are drawn from the beautifully humble life of our Lord and those around Him.

I Must Decrease

Picture this. During the time Jesus walked this earth, John the Baptist became a hugely popular figure in Israel. There hadn't been an authentic God-sent prophet in Israel for more than 400 years. So when John came out of the wilderness preaching fiery sermons and offering a baptism of repentance, the common people and the social outcasts flocked to be near him and be baptized. In fact,

John baptized Jesus! Yet it was John who later said of Jesus and His ministry, "He must increase, but I must decrease" (John 3:30).

John demonstrated the fundamental focus of a Christian's life and ministry: You and I are here to not only reflect Christ but to exalt Him and point others to Him. We are not called to pridefully exalt our ministry, or to hoard a certain ministry or position at church, and especially not at the expense of another person's reputation or usefulness. In fact, we should be on high alert not to allow ourselves to develop a proud, aggressive attitude toward anyone at church or in ministry.

Jealous or bitter rivalry is sinful and divisive. It weakens the unity of the church and leads to ineffective personal ministry. Therefore, refuse to feed a competitive spirit. When someone new with something constructive and helpful to offer arrives on the scene, do what John the Baptist did. Step aside. Move over. Assist in any way you can. Point others to a stronger or better leader—or idea. Get on board. In your heart think, *She must increase, but I must decrease.* You don't have to cease serving, but you should resist the urge to go to the mat fighting to cling to something someone else may be able to do better than you.

Blessed Are the Peacemakers

It's truly tragic when church members squabble. This sinful behavior was condemned for all time in a letter sent to the Philippian church by the apostle Paul. Sadly, two women were named in this factious situation. Paul wrote, "I implore Euodia and I implore Syntyche to be of the same mind in the Lord...help these women" (Philippians 4:2-3). Apparently these women were leading two opposing factions in the church. It's probable their conflict was personal (maybe something as ridiculous and earth-shattering as what color to paint the pastor's office or the women's restroom!). Whatever you do, don't follow in the footsteps of these two women.

======= *Reflecting On Your Heart* =======

It's a beautiful thing to follow Jesus, who said, "Blessed are the peacemakers" (Matthew 5:9). Your calling is to keep your eyes on Jesus, not on those around you. Your focus and purpose is to humbly follow Christ and represent Him faithfully at every opportunity. He is the only one who is to be visible in any ministry you perform or participate in. Seek to reflect Him and His humility. Stay focused on what's truly important— on souls, on spiritual ministry, on kingdom work. The fruit of such a ministry will be God-honoring and positive—not something that's riddled with strife and contention.

Whoever Humbles Himself Will Be Exalted

Jesus often made statements that seemed to be self-contradictory or paradoxical.[8] On one particular occasion, while He was having lunch at a religious leader's house, Jesus noticed how the invited guests were scrambling for the best places at the table. In that culture, the closer a person sat to the host, the greater that guest's position of honor was. The parable Jesus told as a result of what He witnessed was designed to get the guests to think less about their physical and social status and more about spiritual realities (Luke 14:7-10).

In Jesus' story, those who jumped to the front, hoping to be exalted, were instead humiliated when the host asked them to take a lesser seat to make room for some more important guests. Jesus' message was, "Whoever exalts himself will be humbled, and he who humbles himself will be exalted" (verse 11).

A truly humble woman doesn't think too highly of herself...or too lowly either. She simply doesn't think of herself at all—other than to be careful to properly reflect her Savior! Her only thought is how to be of service to others.

So the next time you go to a luncheon, dinner party, potluck, or wedding shower, don't think about who you are. Think instead on who Christ is and how He would act. Meditate on the fact that you are His, that you are His humble disciple. Purpose to assist, serve, and encourage as many as you can...and enjoy the event from the back of the room!

The Lord Looks at the Heart

As we just noted, Jesus was a keen observer of people. He especially liked to sit and watch people in their acts of worship in the temple. These same people became the subjects of some of His stories or parables. One of my favorites shows us what real humility is like. Hear Jesus now as He describes the scene:

> Two men went up to the temple to pray, one a Pharisee and the other a tax collector. The Pharisee stood and prayed thus with himself, "God, I thank You that I am not like other men—extortioners, unjust, adulterers, or even as this tax collector. I fast twice a week; I give tithes of all that I possess." And the tax collector, standing afar off, would not so much as raise his eyes to heaven, but beat his breast, saying, "God, be merciful to me a sinner!" I tell you, this man went down to his house justified rather than the other; for everyone who exalts himself will be humbled, and he who humbles himself will be exalted (Luke 18:10-14).

In this parable, Jesus compared two men. One was outwardly very religious. He seemed to be a humble, God-fearing man. He did all the right things, but his humility was for outward show and attention only. Inside, he was self-righteous and looked down on others, revealing his false humility. By contrast, the inferior, loathed tax collector possessed and displayed a true heart of humility. Jesus said it was this despised man and outcast of society who had truly humbled himself and, as a result, would be exalted.

Unfortunately "man looks at the outward appearance, but the LORD looks at the heart" (1 Samuel 16:7). In God's economy, it's not the mighty and the proud who receive His blessing and approval. No, it's the lowly of mind. Peter, one of the disciples who had personally walked for several years beside Jesus, the ultimate example of humility, described this seeming contradiction in this way: "Be submissive to one another, and be clothed with humility, for God resists the proud, but gives grace to the humble. Therefore humble yourselves under the mighty hand of God, that He may exalt you in due time" (1 Peter 5:5-6).

God isn't telling His people to feel humble. He doesn't even say we're to pray for humility, even though that's not a bad thing to do! No, He's asking us to be humble, to act humbly, to express humility. Jesus put action to His attitude of humility. He willingly served and helped others. And He's asking you and me to join His club, "The Order of the Towel." Read on to learn more about this club.

I Have Given You an Example

As you may know, the land of Palestine is a dry and dusty place today, and it was the same during the time Jesus was on earth. Therefore, when travelers arrived at their destination, they were greeted at the door by a servant who was ready to wash and dry their feet as they entered the house.

In His last hours before His crucifixion, Jesus took His disciples away from the crowds. He wanted to give them a farewell dinner, some parting words of information, advice, and encouragement, and have a time of prayer before His betrayal and arrest. As the disciples entered the upper room they were so busy arguing about which of them would be the greatest in God's kingdom that none of them was willing to stoop down and wash the feet of the others (Luke 22:24).

To their utter shock, Jesus quietly wrapped a towel around His waist, took a basin of water, knelt down, and began to wash and dry each of the disciples' feet (John 13:1-7). Through His actions Jesus modeled Christian humility and began teaching His disciples what it meant to serve selflessly, a lesson He completed with His death on the cross. He instructed His followers to join "The Order of the Towel," saying, "If I then, your Lord and Teacher, have washed your feet, you also ought to wash one another's feet. For I have given you an example, that you should do as I have done to you" (verses 14-15).

This whole episode began with the disciples pridefully arguing over who would have the most prestigious position in Jesus' new kingdom. Jesus' humble service was a complete contrast to their arrogant desire for status. Selfless love and service was a distinctive mark of Jesus' character and is to be mirrored in His true disciples (verses 34-35).

Whenever you feel tempted to think and act pridefully, or you catch yourself desiring a position of honor, stop. In your mind and heart, clothe yourself with humility. Mentally and spiritually put a towel around your waist, get a basin of water, and serve someone. Pray that you become a humble servant to all. Pray for the success of others, especially those you are tempted to envy or put down. And pray daily for a selfless attitude toward those God brings across your path.

Reflecting the Heart of Jesus

How can you reflect a heart of humility? Is it by putting yourself down or by thinking you are of little worth? No, humility is not passive resignation. And it's not the fine art of belittling yourself or others. It comes from knowing Christ and knowing your worth in Him. It takes place in the mind and heart and is referred to as "lowliness of mind" (Philippians 2:3). And it can and should be nurtured and cultivated...and reflected.

A college student asked me, "How can I be more humble?" Believe me, this took some thought. But here are some of the answers I gave her.

Begin each day by reflecting on Christ's great sacrifice on your behalf and considering your own sinfulness. When you follow this pattern, you will be humbled by the grace God has offered to you. Then, in response, humbly thank Jesus for modeling humility.

Next, make willful choices that give humility expression. For instance, talk less and listen more. (And definitely talk less about yourself!) Look for those who are suffering or alone, and reach out. Wherever your day takes you, go to give and to serve as many people as you can. Volunteer to help clean up and set up—to wash feet! Commit yourself to a ministry that no one sees—cooking and baking for others at home, visiting shut-ins and those in hospitals, taking special meals to a cancer victim, cleaning an elderly saint's home.

And here's a biggie! Be a woman of prayer. Everything about prayer breeds humility. The posture of prayer is downward. Talking to God is humbling—He is holy. Worshiping and praising Him is humbling—He is bigger than you. Asking for God's help with your problems and loved ones is humbling—you need His help. Fasting too develops a knowledge of humility. Even the mere act of going without food or missing a meal weakens you physically, not to mention the extended time in prayer that usually accompanies a fast.

Once again, think on Peter's words: "Humble yourselves under the mighty hand of God" (1 Peter 5:6). How many ways can you humble yourself? Each day—and each act and word out of your mouth—is a fresh opportunity to cultivate Jesus' humility as a character quality.

~ A Prayer to Pray ~

Lord, I read about Your humility and I am humbled to the core. Please help me to choose to wrap myself in the garment of humility, to focus not on myself but on others, to consider others as better than myself. Amen.

Joyful

*H*ow would you describe your attitude toward life? Are you the kind of person who sees the glass as half full, or half empty? Of course you know that the reality of the glass of water is both. It's only your perspective that makes the difference.

I've certainly had my share of problems, challenges, and scares in life. And I also have many family members, friends, and acquaintances who have suffered or are presently suffering extreme and continuous pain or heartache, some of them for many years, even decades. Unfortunately some of them are scarred and changed as they've grown bitter or become hardened by their trials. But some are living joyous and productive lives in spite of their chronic pain, ailment, disability, or sorrow.

What makes the difference? This latter group is made up of those who see the "glass" of their life circumstances as not only half full but completely full. In fact, full and overflowing! From their perspective, the positives in their lives far outweigh their infirmities and life condition. And Number One on their list of positives—which they are most happy to share!—is their relationship with God. That's the perspective Isaiah, the great Old Testament prophet, had. He simply could not contain his joy when he thought about all that God had done for him. He wrote,

> I will greatly rejoice in the LORD,
> my soul shall be joyful in my God;
> for He has clothed me with the garments of salvation,

He has covered me with the robe of righteousness
(Isaiah 61:10).

As Christians we have the ultimate reason for rejoicing. No matter what has occurred or is happening to us, we have the ultimate reason for continuous joy because of our relationship with Jesus.

Jesus Shows Us the Way

As you and I come to another character quality on our 30-day journey to becoming more Christlike, we see Jesus as the perfect example of the attitude of joy. He always lived in a complete state of joy regardless of His circumstances. He never allowed emotions to interfere with His joy because it was based on an uninterrupted relationship with His Father.

Here's a startling news flash: Nowhere in the history of Jesus' life, days, and trials recorded in the Bible will you find the word *happiness* used to describe His attitude. And this makes sense, because *happiness* is a term we could never use in relation to Jesus. Why? Because happiness is a response to a sense of well being or good fortune or prosperity. Jesus, as God in human flesh, never allowed Himself to be controlled by His circumstances. He was dependent on the Father to supply whatever resources were needed for the moment. Jesus' joy was a gift from the Father and it transcended any and all the conditions He faced on this earth. And that's a quality we too can possess, and Jesus shows us the way.

Joy No Matter What

The joy Jesus offers is without limit. He offered full joy to His disciples the night before His death by crucifixion. That evening, Jesus shared a Passover meal with them. This group of men had experienced rejection from the religious establishment, death threats, the loss of income, and homelessness during the three years they had followed Jesus. And Jesus, knowing of the betrayal, trial, and sentencing that would come the next morning, wanted to prepare His men for these traumatic events. He reassured them that as they abided in Him and His love, they would always have a special relationship that included the element of joy. He then concluded, "These things I have spoken to you, that My joy may remain in you, and that your joy may be full" (John 15:11). Jesus wanted His disciples (and you!) to know the joy of fellowship with Him—joy to the fullest, without limit, regardless of what was going on in their lives.

No One Will Take Your Joy from You

During this same Passover meal, Jesus also clearly told His confused disciples that in a little while He would be leaving them, referring to His death by crucifixion. But He also had incredibly good news. They would see Him again, referring to His resurrection from the dead (John 16:16-19). Yes, they would be sad, but when He appeared again they would have great joy!

At this point Jesus used an illustration most women can relate to, that of childbirth. He explained there is real pain during labor, but that pain is quickly forgotten in the joy of the birth of a child. Jesus then applied the illustration by reassuring His men, "You now have sorrow; but I will see you again and your heart will rejoice, and your joy no one will take from you" (John 16:22). Joy, genuine joy, is lasting and has its source in Jesus. The disciples and all believers throughout time, including you, would have Jesus' joy because He would be with them permanently through the Holy Spirit.

Ask...That Your Joy May Be Full

After reassuring the disciples of the joy that would be theirs through the Spirit's presence in them, Jesus gave them one final promise of a joyful life: Their joy would continue in answered prayer. To encourage them in the habit of prayer, Jesus explained, "Until now you have asked nothing in My name. Ask, and you will receive, that your joy may be full" (verse 24). Their joy would always be available as they prayed and then received answers consistent with Jesus' purposes in their lives.

===== *Reflecting On Your Heart* =====

Joy comes from having a consistent relationship with Jesus. As you "walk in the Spirit" (Galatians 5:16), your life is vitally connected with Jesus. Then, no matter what you are suffering or enduring, no matter what your lacks and losses are, the Lord will help you have joy as you go through the difficult times. His joy will keep you from sinking into depression or succumbing to discouragement. Stay close to Jesus and He will keep you on an even keel, no matter how overwhelming or devastating your circumstances. As Jesus promised, "Your heart will rejoice, and your joy no one will take from you" (John 16:22).

The Joy That Was Set Before Jesus

In crucifixion, the Romans had developed the ultimate instrument for torture and pain. The Roman cross was feared by both criminals and law-abiding people. To the Romans the cross was a symbol of suffering, but because of Jesus' death, the cross now symbolizes salvation. In His gruesome death by crucifixion, Jesus provides us with the supreme model of joy in the midst of a most horrible experience. The writer of the book of Hebrews helps us to look to "Jesus, the author and finisher of our faith, who for the joy that was set before Him endured the cross, despising the shame, and has sat down at the right hand of the throne of God" (Hebrews 12:2).

Knowing His sacrifice and suffering would result in great joy, Jesus focused on His future with the Father as He endured the pain of death. He never lost sight of the joy that He had in His relationship with the Father.

Reflecting On Your Heart

How do you normally approach or go through your difficult times? Is it with dread? Fear? Anger? Complaining? Tears? Sighs? Resignation? Why go through such emotions when this amazing quality of joy that Jesus experienced in His darkest hour is also available

to you? Won't you look to Jesus for this joy? Let Him
help you endure your darkest hours and your most
painful days with pure, full, indescribable joy.

Hannah Shows Us the Way

What a treat God gives us by showing us the gallant life of one
of His women, Hannah. She was persecuted, put down, and picked
on...and all of this while her heart was breaking. She shared her
husband with another woman. And if that wasn't bad enough, the
other wife had children while poor Hannah didn't. And to make
her life even more miserable, the other woman provoked and rid-
iculed Hannah because of her inability to have children.

How did Hannah handle all of these heartaches? She bore her
pain in silent sorrow, sharing it only with God when she "prayed
to the LORD and wept in anguish" (1 Samuel 1:10). When her time
of prayer ended, she offered up this praise: "My heart rejoices in
the LORD...I rejoice in Your salvation" (1 Samuel 2:1).

Hannah teaches us some powerful means for dealing with suffering. Several times in this book I point out that problems are a
part of life. Hannah had problems, and so do you and every other
person alive. That's because we live in a sinful and fallen world in
which we will be hurt by others and we ourselves will also hurt
others. And we'll suffer physically as our imperfect bodies dete-
riorate and fall prey to sickness and disease. But through it all—
whatever trouble we encounter—we can pray for the grace to do
as Hannah did:

⌐ She kept her suffering to herself rather than fight back, whine,
or complain to anyone who would listen.

⌐ She took her deepest sorrows to the right person—to God
Himself.

⌐ She prayed and wept before the Lord and rose up, "and her
face was no longer sad" (1 Samuel 1:18).

～ She brought the problem of her barrenness to God in earnest prayer and with a vow.

～ She praised the Lord for the joy she had in Him and in His salvation.

The Bible Shows Us the Way

Who wouldn't want joy instead of the draining, negative alternatives? The good news is that you and I can cultivate this bright and precious character quality. The Bible shows us how. Consider these changes you can make in your endeavor to experience joy even while you are under the stress of suffering.

～ Take joy in your salvation. "My soul shall be joyful in the LORD; it shall rejoice in His salvation" (Psalm 35:9).

～ Walk in the Spirit. "The fruit of the Spirit is...joy" (Galatians 5:22).

～ Choose to respond in joy. "Count it all joy when you fall into various trials" (James 1:2).

～ Offer up praise to God. "Let us continually offer the sacrifice of praise to God, that is, the fruit of our lips, giving thanks to His name" (Hebrews 13:15).

～ Understand God's will regarding thanksgiving. "In everything give thanks; for this is the will of God in Christ Jesus for you" (1 Thessalonians 5:18).

～ Pray for joy in your ordeals. "Until now you have asked nothing in My name. Ask, and you will receive, that your joy may be full" (John 16:24).

Reflecting the Heart of Jesus

The purpose of this book is to take a good look at the character traits that stand out in Jesus' life. Our hearts' desire is to follow in His steps, to emulate Him, to grow and become more like Him. Our dear Savior suffered worse than any person throughout all time has ever suffered. We read of His pain and agony...and yet we read of His sheer joy!

Here's an exercise that might reveal a lot about your joy quotient. Chart out your emotional state for the past few months on a piece of graph paper. Label the bottom of the paper "depression" and the top "euphoria." What would your graph look like? Would it depict great peaks of giddiness when all was going well? And would it show deep valleys of sadness when things were not going so well? Why the dramatic mood shifts? Maybe your response to trials and problems was so varied and inconsistent because there were times when you took your eyes off Jesus.

Jesus offers you His solution to your mood swings. He will give you His joy as you choose to work on a more consistent relationship with Him. And you can nurture that friendship. You can think on Him more frequently. You can rehearse His promises. You can look heavenward and think upward thoughts instead of viewing your situation through worldly, negative eyes. And you can pray instead of losing heart (Luke 18:1).

If you are prone to responses that fail to bring you God's joy in your unjoyful situations, take positive action. Decide not to allow misfortune or fortune to move you up and down the mood scale. The joy of living close to Jesus and drawing on His strength each day—even moment by moment—will keep you levelheaded, hold you steady, rein in your emotions, and cause you to rejoice always regardless of what's happening around you.

⌐ A Prayer to Pray ⌐

Dear Jesus, help me to remember that my joy comes from my relationship and walk with You. You are my joy and the source of my joy. May I stop allowing anyone or anything to rob me of my joy in You, and may others see Your joy in me. Amen.

Kind

*K*indness seems to be an endangered species as a character quality. To be sure, there are random acts of kindness all around us. But in general, and if you watch or listen to the news, you are probably convinced that we live in a very mean world. I did, however, recently hear a bit of encouraging news. It seems some students attending a Seattle-area grade school that was experiencing problems with bullying started a "kindness club." The kids write notes of kindness and thank yous for acts of kindness they received or saw done to others. The notes were then linked together to form a chain. Amazingly, "the chain of kindness" grew to run the length of all the school hallways…and back! That would be an astonishing story by itself, but what's even more fantastic is that their example has inspired other schools to start similar clubs.

Example is a powerful tool in effecting a change in behavior. And there's no greater example to look to when it comes to kindness than to Jesus, the Lord Himself.

God Shows Us the Way

God is often pictured as a God of wrath and vengeance. Critics love to depict Him as a cruel and vengeful deity. But in reality, the character of God is just the opposite. In the Old Testament, the man Jonah knew kindness was a part of God's true nature. God asked Jonah to go to one of the most barbarous and brutal nations of his day and offer them God's salvation. Jonah's response to God's request? He started an ocean journey in the opposite direction to avoid going to Assyria and its capital city, Nineveh. After getting thrown overboard and spending three days in the stomach of a great fish, Jonah reluctantly went to Nineveh.

When the people of Nineveh heard Jonah's warnings of judgment, there was a great revival. Wouldn't you think Jonah would have been happy? But he wasn't. He wanted God to judge the people. He then gave God this reason for his initial hesitancy in going to Nineveh: "I fled...for I know that You are a gracious and merciful God, slow to anger and abundant in lovingkindness, One who relents from doing harm" (Jonah 4:2).

In the New Testament, the apostle Paul also testified of God's kindness. In his letter to the Christians in Rome, Paul wrote of "the riches of His kindness and tolerance and patience," explaining that "the kindness of God leads [one] to repentance" (Romans 2:4 NASB). Think on it! Your salvation is a direct result of the kindness of God.

And in his epistle to the Ephesian church, Paul wrote about God's act of making those who are spiritually dead alive in Christ. He wanted believers to know that one reason for God's salvation of sinners was that "in the ages to come He might show the exceeding riches of His grace in His kindness toward us in Christ Jesus" (Ephesians 2:7).

Reflecting On Your Heart

God's great heart is a heart filled and overflowing with kindness. It is this kindness of God that moved Him to extend the grace of His salvation to you. What is an appropriate heart response to such truth? Worship. Praise. Thanksgiving. And kindness. God extended and demonstrated His kindness to you, and you in turn should reach out and demonstrate His kindness to others. You are to become a link in His eternal "chain of kindness"!

Jesus Shows Us the Way

As you can tell, kindness is the next quality in our meditations on Christlike character. As always, Jesus set the bar, as He radiated pure kindness. In fact, Jesus was "the kindness...of God" (Titus 3:4), who appeared in human flesh and moved among His creation reaching out in acts of kindness whenever and wherever He saw a need. Jesus was benevolence in action. Sympathy was so much a part of His nature that He simply could not turn away from anyone who was suffering. Kindness then, as exemplified by Jesus, desires to do something about what it sees as a need.

Nowhere in the Bible will you see the word *nice* used to describe the character of Jesus. While a nice person may appear polite, it's possible for that person to merely be acting in a superficial way. That's why *nice* doesn't qualify as a true character quality. Kindness, on the other hand, does speak to character. A kind person is caring, sympathetic, and considerate. And a kind person's actions are sincere and deeply intense. As you read through the life of Jesus you can't miss this quality lived out in His deeds. Here are a few instances in which Jesus acted with graciousness and affection—with kindness.

What Great Things the Lord Has Done for You

The demon-possessed man—One of the classic accounts of Jesus' mercy was the time when He cast out demons from a man who called himself "Legion" because he was possessed by so many demons. Talk about a man who was in pain and agony! He...

> had his dwelling among the tombs; and no one could bind him, not even with chains, because he had often been bound with shackles and chains. And the chains had been pulled apart by him, and the shackles broken in pieces; neither could anyone tame him. And always, night and day, he was in the mountains and in the tombs, crying out and cutting himself with stones (Mark 5:3-5).

This tortured man was a pathetic sight. No one could get near him because he was so violent. But Jesus cast out the demons, sending them into a herd of swine. Jesus then sent the man back to his home to broadcast to others about the kindness he had experienced. Jesus told him to "go home to your friends, and tell them what great things the Lord has done for you, and how He has had compassion on you" (Mark 5:19).

Reflecting On Your Heart

"Tell them what great things the Lord has done for you." Those words were an assignment given from the Lord to a man who had been helpless and without hope— that is, before Jesus set him free. Almost the exact same words were offered to God as praise from the lips of Mary, the mother of Jesus, in her famous prayer known as Mary's Magnificat. She prayed, "He who is mighty has done great things for me" (Luke 1:49). In her prayer, Mary rejoiced in God, her Savior (verse 47). If God is your Savior, you already know in your heart what great things He has done for you. In His kindness He has saved you from a life without hope and set you free. Follow Jesus' instructions to the man who had been filled with demons. Go to your family and friends—and anyone else who will listen—and tell them what great things the Lord has done for you, and how He has had compassion on you.

Go and Sin No More

The woman caught in adultery—God hates sin. Yet in His love He took the ultimate action and sent His Son to die for the penalty of sin. Jesus never condoned sin, but He loved sinners. On one occasion the religious leaders tried to trap Jesus by bringing before Him a woman who had been caught in adultery. (You can read the details in John 8:1-11.) The Jewish law required stoning the woman. But Roman law had forbidden stoning as a capital offense. Sadly, these men, in their hatred for Jesus, were attempting to use this poor woman to discredit Him.

Without speaking a word, Jesus wrote something in the sand for all the woman's accusers to see. Maybe it was a list of the sins these men had committed. No one knows. But whatever it was, Jesus said to the accusers, "He who is without sin among you, let him throw a stone at her first" (verse 7). Slowly, one by one, all the religious leaders quietly slipped away, leaving the woman alone with Jesus. He asked, "'Woman, where are those accusers of yours? Has no one condemned you?' She said, 'No one, Lord'" (verses 10-11). Kindly Jesus said, "Neither do I condemn you; go and sin no more" (verse 11).

What a kind Savior we have! The world is quick to judge, but Jesus is quick to forgive. Let's not tread on His kindness. Instead, let's make the effort to "go and sin no more."

He Put His Hands on His Eyes

The blind man—When you think of a kind person, what singular act usually demonstrates that person's concern? It's a touch, right? A hug. A pat on the back. Jesus healed many who were blind, but on one occasion, the Bible shows Jesus' attention directed toward a particular blind man. You can picture Jesus' kindness as "He took the blind man by the hand and led him out of the town… He put His hands on his eyes again and made him look up. And he was restored and saw everyone clearly" (Mark 8:23,25).

Are you experiencing the kind "touch" of Jesus? Ask for it—it's only a prayer away!

He Took Them Up in His Arms

The little children—When you enter a children's classroom at your church, what picture is often hanging on the wall? When I was a child, I saw a picture of Jesus holding one or two young children in His lap while others huddled around Him, leaning on Him, touching Him, resting at His feet. I can still see it in my mind as I'm remembering it.

Now imagine this: Jesus' disciples trying to keep a group of children away from Him. This really happened! And what did our warmhearted Savior say and do?

> When Jesus saw it, He was greatly displeased and
> said to them, "Let the little children come to Me, and

do not forbid them; for of such is the kingdom of God."...And He took them up in His arms, laid His hands on them, and blessed them (Mark 10:14,16).

───────────── *Reflecting On Your Heart* ─────────────

Jesus loved, welcomed, enjoyed, and blessed the children. Others rebuked them and tried to push them away, but the Lord of kindness valued them. He in no way viewed their presence as an intrusion on His space. And He in no way wanted to hinder them from coming to Him, the Christ. If you're a mom who desires to reflect Jesus' kindness, start with the little—or big— ones right under your own roof. Pray and purpose to make it clear to your kids that they are cherished, a priority to you, and a joy to your heart. And most of all, dedicate your life to bringing them to Jesus.

Women in the Bible Show Us the Way

One of my lifelong studies has been the women of the Bible. They—and their many acts of kindness—have been cataloged and kept forever on the pages of Scripture. My mind is running wild as I think immediately of scores of these women who lived out the kindness of God toward others. Enjoy these few and read with an open heart, a heart like they possessed.

He Can Turn in Here

The Shunammite woman (2 Kings 4:8-10)—In the Old Testament we find the example of a woman who saw a need...and acted. She observed that the prophet Elisha passed by on a regular basis. She also noticed that he didn't seem to have a place to eat. What did this lady's kindness do? She took action and "she persuaded him to eat some food" with her family anytime he came her way (verse 8). She also noticed that Elisha didn't have a place to stay. Again, what did her kindness do? She asked her husband if they could build a little "prophet's chamber" above their home so Elisha would have a place to stay anytime he passed by or came to town. As she appealed to her husband, "so it will be, whenever he comes to us, he can turn in there" (verse 10).

This woman's eyes were open to the needs of another, and so was her heart. Because of the kindness of one woman, God's servant had two less things to worry about as he traveled and proclaimed truth about the Lord God. He had food to eat and a place to lay his head.

Abounding with Deeds of Kindness

The disciple named Dorcas (Acts 9:36-41)—In the New Testament another kind woman named Dorcas (also translated Tabitha) noticed the needs of others. Luke, the writer of the book of Acts, reported that "this woman was abounding with deeds of kindness and charity which she continually did" (verse 36 NASB). Among her kind deeds was sewing tunics and garments for the widows. Dorcus had noticed that the widows had a need—clothing—and she acted. She lived out James's description of "pure and undefiled religion"—she visited the widows in their trouble and tended to their needs (James 1:27).

Be Kind to One Another

Both the nameless Shunammite woman and Dorcas show us kindness. And God's desire that we be kind has not changed through the centuries. As the apostle Paul wrote in the New Testament to you and me and all believers, "Be kind to one another, tenderhearted" (Ephesians 4:32).

Being kind is not something you can fabricate. You can make an effort to be nice, and that's helpful. But kindness comes from a deep and abiding relationship with Jesus. It's a heart attitude, a spiritual condition. It's also a fruit of the Spirit (Galatians 5:22-23). When you walk with Jesus, you will show kindness. Your heart will be filled with compassion. And you'll be sensitive to the tremendous needs in the people around you. Like Jesus, you will show kindness not only to the poor and helpless, but to anyone who is hurting. You will become the...

> eyes for the elderly,
>> ears for the suffering,
>>> legs for the lame,
>>>> hands for the sick, and a
>>>>> shoulder for the brokenhearted.

Reflecting the Heart of Jesus

God, in His very nature, is kind. He responds to those who call on His name, including you. He is sympathetic to your situation and tender, warmhearted, and forbearing when it comes to your life and actions. As the Son of God, Jesus mirrored the Father and desires that you mirror Him too.

To accurately reflect Him, Jesus calls you to move away from the socially acceptable attitude of being nice to people. He has much greater plans for you—a life "abounding with deeds of kindness and charity" (Acts 9:36). He desires in you a heart filled with a real, sincere kindness that goes beyond pretense and politeness. A simple act of thoughtfulness on your part can become an extraordinary blessing for the one receiving it...and for you. Kindness is a characteristic of one of God's people, and when you're kind, you display the character of Christ to a watching world, allowing others to catch a glimpse of Jesus.

~ A Prayer to Pray ~

Dear Jesus, my "wish list" is long! I desire with all my heart to live a life of kindness, to imitate Your compassion, benevolence, and forgiving attitude. Create in me a sympathy for those who are less fortunate, who are in pain or need. And may You, Lord Jesus, be exalted with each act of kindness done in Your name. Amen.

Loving

*C*an you pinpoint several "most important days" of your life? For us Christians, the day we believe in Jesus is definitely the singular most important day, standing far and above any and every other experience. Nothing else in life will ever come close in comparison to the day you inherited eternal life, had your sins forgiven, and entered into a relationship with God. Beyond this most important day, those who are married usually point to their wedding date. This red-letter day is always remembered by an attentive and loving husband who makes it a special day with a special meal at a special restaurant. (Well, at least that's the dream!)

Would you believe today is my anniversary! Jim and I met at the University of Oklahoma on a blind date, fell instantly and hopelessly in love, and were married eight months later. If you'd pressed us to define love back then, we would have given you a far different definition than what we would give these many years later. What accounts for the difference in the *then* and *now* definitions? Time. Struggles. Adversity. Physical, mental, and spiritual growth. Those are only a few of the reasons our definition of love is vastly different today.

Love is one of the most misunderstood emotions, attitudes, and qualities that we as humans desire and possess. The world wants to define love as some sort of physical attraction to the exclusion of just about everything else. But the Bible has another way of looking at love and measuring it. Furthermore, it features the perfect person to demonstrate God's definition of love—Jesus Christ.

Before we learn about love from Jesus, let's see how the Bible describes love from the perspective of God the Father. As with many of the qualities we're looking at throughout this book, love is both a divine quality within the nature of the Trinity as well as an activity each member of the Trinity performs. For instance, here are some facts about God's love:

- God's love is part of His nature—"God is love" (1 John 4:8).

- God's love for the Son is from all eternity—from "before the foundation of the world" (John 17:24).

- God's love is active—"He gave His only begotten Son" (John 3:16).

- God's love is enduring—"Neither death...nor any other...thing shall be able to separate us from the love of God" (see Romans 8:35-39).

- God's love includes those who are lost—"The Son of Man has come to seek and to save that which was lost" (Luke 19:10).

- God's love is sacrificial—"He...did not spare His own Son, but delivered Him up for us all" (Romans 8:32).

- God's love blesses His children—"What manner of love the Father has bestowed on us, that we should be called children of God" (1 John 3:1).

- God's love is everlasting—"I have loved you with an everlasting love" (Jeremiah 31:3).

Jesus Shows Us the Way

In Jesus we find both the greatest model of love and our ultimate resource for loving others. Jesus was perfect love in human flesh. He loved perfectly, and He teaches—and commands—us to do the same. Hear now the Master Teacher's instruction on love!

Jesus' Teachings on Love

Love chooses God as first priority—"'You shall love the LORD your God with all your heart, with all your soul, and with all your mind.' This is the first and great commandment" (Matthew 22:37-38).

Love chooses others as the next priority—"And the second is like it: 'You shall love your neighbor as yourself'" (verse 39).

Love chooses to obey Jesus—"If you love Me, keep My commandments" (John 14:15). "If anyone loves Me, he will keep My word" (verse 23). "If you keep My commandments, you will abide in My love" (John 15:10).

Love chooses to follow Jesus' example and command to love others— "A new commandment I give to you, that you love one another; as I have loved you, that you also love one another" (John 13:34).

Love chooses to forgive rather than seek revenge—"Love your enemies, bless those who curse you, do good to those who hate you, and pray for those who spitefully use you and persecute you" (Matthew 5:43-44).

Jesus' Practice of Love

Because He perfectly practiced love, Jesus shows us how to do the same and live out His commands that we "love one another" (John 13:34).

Jesus loved His friends—Martha, Mary, and Lazarus were three of Jesus' closest friends, and we read that "Jesus loved Martha and her sister and Lazarus" (John 11:5). We see Him in their home having meals on several occasions and arriving to offer His help after Lazarus's death.[9]

Can you imagine having Jesus in your home not only as an honored guest but also as one who visibly shows love toward you? Friends are a gift from God and should be treated with love and respect. As a friend, Jesus was there when this family needed Him in a life-or-death crisis. He came to Martha and Mary in their hour of need even though the local religious leaders were seeking ways to kill Him. His love for His friends outweighed His concerns for His safety.

=========== *Reflecting On Your Heart* ===========

It's easy to love friends who return love. Friendships are also easy to maintain when little is required from you. But what about times of need? Are you still there for your friends when they ask for your help? And what if that help is needed for a while, even a long while? The mark of a true friend is persistent love, regardless of any burdens the friendship presents.

Jesus loved His fellow workers—John, who is referred to as the disciple "whom Jesus loved" (John 13:23), gives this insight into the love Jesus had for His 12 colaborers: "When Jesus knew that His hour had come that He should depart from this world to the Father, having loved His own who were in the world, He loved them to the end" (John 13:1). To the end! Loving your family and friends is one thing, but how about those you work with every day, or those you minister alongside at church each week? How are your relationships with them? They can be a bit of a challenge at times, can't they?

Speaking of a challenge, try to imagine the God of creation, the Sovereign of the world, having to babysit a group made up of mostly fishermen from a backwater part of a tiny country in the midst of a great big world. Surely there had to be more interesting, more educated, more "with it" people to spend time with than these guys! If this had been your assignment, what attitudes do you think you might have shown toward these men? Impatience? Disgust? Disrespect? Irritation? These men never quite understood Jesus' mission until He rose from the grave. And yet the Bible states that "He loved them to the end" (John 13:1), even though He knew they would doubt, desert, deny, and betray Him.

=========== *Reflecting On Your Heart* ===========

What a beautiful example to follow! The next time you catch yourself about to respond with impatience, irritation, or disgust over something one of your workmates or acquaintances or colaborers at church does or doesn't do, or maybe something about them that bugs you to no end, remember Jesus. Focus on understanding and appreciating that person and her point of reference. Above all, love her with Christ's love. And remember, "love will cover a multitude of sins" (1 Peter 4:8).

Jesus loved the lost—Jesus' mission on earth is described in this verse: "The Son of Man has come to seek and to save that which was lost" (Luke 19:10). So it's not surprising to see Jesus actively mingling with the lost. In the chapter on generosity, we met a young man who approached Jesus. If you recall, he was very wealthy, young, and a ruler. He came to Jesus to ask how to "inherit eternal life."[10]

How many people do you think crossed Jesus' path with a question, a need, a complaint on a daily basis? We might think that after a while, Jesus could have become a little jaded and calloused, wishing for a break from the multitudes of people who approached Him. Then we remember, "But this is Jesus! Of course He would always respond with 100 percent pure Godlike love!" And sure enough, in the middle of His conversation with this young ruler, the Bible says, "Then Jesus, looking at him, loved him" (verse 21). What tender, straightforward, moving, understandable words—Jesus loved him! Jesus knew the man wasn't willing to follow Him, so He gave the man one last test: "Go your way, sell whatever you have and give to the poor...take up the cross, and follow Me" (verse 21).

Reflecting On Your Heart

You are probably surrounded by unbelievers, by people like the rich young ruler. It's easy to look upon them as "the enemy." They don't share your values, nor do they desire them or respect them. They don't talk and act like you do, and there's no way they want to! Maybe your natural response is to feel ill at ease when you're around non-Christians, to even try to avoid any contact with them. Yet Jesus shows us a better way—His way. Jesus accepted the young man the way he was. He asked for a commitment, but He never said or did anything harsh toward the man. He perfectly modeled the attitude you're to have toward the lost. They can't act any other way because "the natural man does not receive the things of the Spirit of God" (1 Corinthians 2:14). Since they are not Christians, remember, they aren't the enemy. They are only victims of the enemy. Do as Jesus did. Look at them... and love them.

Jesus' Love Was Sacrificial

Jesus took love to its ultimate test when He willingly went to the cross to secure our salvation. He provided the greatest example ever of unselfish and sacrificial love. Jesus was speaking of Himself when He said, "Greater love has no one than this, than to lay down one's life for his friends" (John 15:13).

Love is costly. Love asks something from you. Hopefully you won't be asked to die for someone, but Christ's love asks you to practice sacrificial love in some very practical ways...such as listening, helping, serving, encouraging, and giving of your time and money.

Where does sacrificial love begin? With a relationship with God through Jesus Christ. Once you are a child of God, spending time with God in His Word and prayer stirs and refreshes love each new day. From there love moves out in loving attitudes and actions toward your family first, then flows to other believers, and finally to the world, to any and all who cross your path. Because of the indwelling Holy Spirit, you have God's love to give! Just be sure you follow Jesus' command to love God first and then love others: "This commandment we have from Him: that he who loves God must love his brother also" (1 John 4:21).

Reflecting the Heart of Jesus

Have you ever thought about why Jesus commands you to love? Love requires something of you. It takes effort. And sadly, love is not always a normal response, unless perhaps you're a mother. But beyond this familial bond, love must be nurtured. It must be nudged a bit, especially if you are hesitating when it comes to reaching out in love, maybe because you were hurt at some time as you tried loving another person.

If for some reason or other you find yourself hesitant to obey God's command to love, you need to recall how deeply you are loved by Jesus in spite of your sins and faults. His unconditional love should move you to love others. It shows you the way to love. Realizing how much God loves you will begin to remove your difficulties in loving others. Then, as you practice love toward others, the feelings of love will follow naturally. You'll find yourself reflecting the heart of Jesus as you reach out in love—just like He did.

⌒ A Prayer to Pray ⌒

My precious Jesus, I thank You for the gift of love You extended to me in salvation—a gift I could not earn and can never repay. And Holy Spirit, I thank You that You teach me about love and prompt me, encourage me, and enable me to love others. And I thank You, Father, that I can love You because You first loved me. Amen.

Patient

*P*atience is a virtue."

"I want patience...and I want it now!"

"Patience is a bitter plant that produces sweet fruit."

You've probably heard or read most of those axioms before. And you probably desire—and need—the "sweet fruit" of patience as a part of your daily life.

As a woman, you need patience in your relationships and your life situation. If you're married, you need patience with your husband. You and your spouse are each different and yet you must live day by day under the same roof. Or, I know many military wives who must live patiently day by day for months or even a year or more without their husband. And if you have children, probably each and every minute of your life calls for patience! And then there are those in the workplace, the neighborhood, and your extended family. The list of relationships that require patience certainly goes on!

So, if your past 24-hour span was anything like mine, trials, situations, and even a few irritating people dotted the day you laid at God's feet early in the morning. Your fervent prayer was that God would help you to live this one day for Him, by Him, through Him, and to Him. You so wanted to respond to the events of the day with His grace, like He would, and reflect Him to others.

Well, certainly we should begin our days with such a prayer, such a heart's desire. There's nothing wrong and everything right about wanting to live for and like Jesus. That's the goal of our every day!

Jesus Shows Us the Way

As we continue to admire the magnificent qualities Jesus possessed, qualities we want to emulate as well, we can look to Jesus for patience. Yet it's so hard to be patient when we have unpleasant encounters and meet up with situations and people who would try the patience of just about anyone. So, what did Jesus show and tell us about patience when it comes to difficult people and circumstances? We need to know...and we need to know right now!

How Often Shall I Forgive?

Here's a little test: How patient are you with the faults of others? Maybe someone owes you some money. Or their fault could be their behavior, such as lying, using bad language, or their habit of putting you down. And maybe they come to you and ask you to please be patient, promising they'll pay you back, or change their behavior, or mend their ways. And maybe this happens over and over again!

What's your patience quotient when you are repeatedly wronged by someone? Could you patiently forgive and accept a person after the first offence? And the second? And on and on and on? We've seen this example before in this book, but let's revisit Jesus' question-and-answer session with His disciple Peter. This time, let's view the scene through the lens of patience. What does Jesus say we're to do when we're wronged? When Peter "came to Him and said, 'Lord, how often shall my brother sin against me, and I forgive him? Up to seven times?' Jesus said to him, 'I do not say to you, up to seven times, but up to seventy times seven'" (Matthew 18:21-23).

Forgiveness is one way of showing patience toward the shortcomings of others. Jesus asks you and me to remain patient with others who have sinned against us. To be ready to forgive those who have wronged us, we must learn to deal with them "in a spirit of gentleness" (Galatians 6:1).

A Right Response to Abuse

Verbal abuse is tough to take! People can use language in cruel and hurtful ways. Words can devastate and spark strong emotions in us. Your first natural—and fleshly—response might be to lash out with your own stream of harsh words. It's easy to open your mouth and spew out awful verbiage in return. You may even try to justify such behavior by saying someone else started it. You may try telling yourself you'll feel better after you vent some steam or let that person know exactly how you feel or what you think. And you may even find yourself tempted to do something worse, like lashing out physically. But you and I both know that lashing out either verbally or physically is not the response Jesus wants from us. He shows us another way, the best way—His way, a way that reflects Him and accurately represents Him.

During the early morning before His crucifixion, the 100 percent perfect and sinless Jesus was paraded before several religious and political groups. His first encounter was with a religious group that included the high priest and scribes and elders. They attempted to bring false charges against Jesus. Finally, in desperation, they produced several witnesses who gave false or at least distorted testimony against Jesus. Throughout the proceedings, Jesus kept silent (Matthew 26:57-63).

What was the source of Jesus' patience while He was verbally abused and mistreated? Peter described the Lord's response this way: He "committed no sin, nor was deceit found in His mouth," and "when He was reviled, [He] did not revile in return; when He suffered, He did not threaten, but committed Himself to Him who judges righteously" (1 Peter 2:22-23). Rather than lash back, Jesus committed Himself to the Father.

Reflecting On Your Heart

Looking to God through prayer is always the best response to any difficult situation. This first move gives you time to discern the right way to handle a problem, and helps you practice patience while you pray and seek God's guidance. It keeps you from giving in to your initial impulse to lash out. It's impossible to pray and return an abuse at the same time. Prayer will allow you to commit yourself and the situation into God's hands.

Your silent response and patience in the face of unjust criticism, blaming, or misunderstanding bears much fruit. And it gives glory and honor to God. As Peter explains, "When you do good and suffer, if you take it patiently, this is commendable before God. For to this you were called, because Christ also suffered for us, leaving us an example, that you should follow His steps" (verses 20-21).

Love Your Enemies

Jesus, the Master Teacher, also instructs us regarding patience in relationships, especially with problem people—even those He labels as enemies. He says you are to "love your enemies." Then He explains how this is done: "Pray for those who mistreat you" (Luke 6:27-28 NIV).

It's clear that as Christians you and I are not to return "evil for evil or reviling for reviling, but on the contrary blessing" (1 Peter 3:9). What Jesus expects from us instead is the godly response of patience, and prayer is the perfect picture of patience in action. He wants us to do nothing in fleshly response toward our enemies, toward those who hurt us in some way. Instead, we're to give a blessing and pray. Isn't that exactly what Jesus did when He prayed for those who nailed Him to the cross? "Father, forgive them; for they do not know what they do" (Luke 23:34). So pray for the difficult people in your life. Ask God to fill you with His patience. Use your heart for prayer, not hatred.

But One Thing Is Needed

Like me, I'm sure you've been guilty of being short with people because of a pressure situation. When I'm under pressure, it can cause me to be impatient with myself, my schedule, my commitments...and anyone who dares to come near me! And I know I'm not alone, because there's a woman in the Bible who did the same thing. Fortunately my impatience hasn't been forever documented on paper like Martha's episode was (see Luke 10:38-42).

Jesus and His disciples had "dropped in" to Mary's house for what I'm sure everyone hoped would be a nice quiet dinner and a time to rest and relax and replenish their bodies and minds. But this didn't happen because, in the midst of preparing the meal, Martha noticed that her sister, Mary, was missing.

As Martha rounded the corner from the kitchen, she spotted Mary just sitting(!) at the feet of Jesus, listening to Him teach. Well, Martha cracked and burst into the room full of guests and practically demanded that Jesus give Mary a good scolding for not helping her in the kitchen. Martha's impatience caused her to lash out at her sister and accuse Jesus of not caring about her and her service in the kitchen.

However, rather than scold Mary, Jesus patiently explained to Martha what was truly important—tending to spiritual needs over physical needs. He said, "You are worried and troubled about many things. But one thing is needed, and Mary has chosen that good part, which will not be taken away from her" (verses 41-42).

Reflecting On Your Heart

> So often impatience is the result of choosing to do things in the flesh, in your own strength. You get impatient or frustrated with yourself or someone else because your plan for the day, or the event, or the pattern of your life, seems to slam into a roadblock. Your dreams just aren't coming true. Others seem to fail you, and you find yourself alone and trying to pick up the pieces of a project or goal. Jesus is telling you, as He told Martha, to refocus on what's really important: your relationship with Him. Be patient! Calm down! Slow down! Cease striving! Take time to stop all your busy activity and sit down. Look to Jesus, your wonderful, patient, kind, wise Lord. Hear His voice. Center on Him. Recall His life and the Scriptures that reveal Him. And pray.

The Judge Is Standing at the Door!

One evening while a group of us women were studying about patience, we came across an encouraging passage written by James to a group of poor and abused Christians. What would you advise such sufferers to do? James told these oppressed readers to "be patient, brethren, until the coming of the Lord. See how the farmer waits for the precious fruit of the earth, waiting patiently for it until it receives the early and latter rain. You also be patient. Establish your hearts, for the coming of the Lord is at hand" (James 5:7-8).

At first glance my group wasn't sure what all of this meant. But we read on to verse 9: "Behold, the Judge is standing at the door!" After some digging we finally began to understand the connection: The Lord is coming, and the Lord is the Judge. When He arrives He will judge all things and all people, including those who persecute and oppress us. That's His role and His job. Until the wondrous event of the Lord's arrival, our role and our job is to remain patient with our life situation and spend our energies building our trust in the Lord.

Is your heart crying out, "Come quickly, Lord Jesus"? If so, there's nothing wrong with that. When the Lord and Judge arrives on the scene, He will make all things right. Oppression will come to an end. Our suffering will end as we enjoy the continuing presence of Jesus. Not only that, but the Lord will reward us for our patience with difficult people. And He will punish our enemies, judging appropriately and correcting abuses. So we are to patiently endure any suffering we face because the Lord, the Judge, has promised to return and make things right.

Reflecting On Your Heart

Ask yourself, "Can I wait?" The Bible says you can and you must. So pick the person in your life who has caused or is causing you the most personal pain—the person who is hostile, mean, ungrateful, or who ignores you, insults you, slanders you, or blocks your progress. Before the Lord—the Judge— pray for God's grace and His help to resist every urge to retaliate or punish that person. Instead, in patience, do nothing while you wait. Wait on the Lord, wait for the Judge!

Walk in the Spirit

Life is not simple, and that's an understatement! There's not a day that goes by in my life (and I would imagine in yours as well) when there isn't a problem that requires patience. What's your patience level while stuck in a traffic jam? Or how do you hold up while waiting eagerly for something good (like conceiving a long-awaited and wanted baby), or waiting in despair for something bad (like the inevitable death of a parent or loved one who is in the process of dying)? Patience is the capacity to tolerate delay, trouble, or suffering without becoming angry or upset and blowing your top! When we're faced with challenges, patience is not usually our normal first response. How can we change that?

The answer is the Holy Spirit. Jesus promised to send a helper, the Holy Spirit, to come alongside and dwell with and in all who believe in Him (John 14:15-17). It is the Spirit who enables you and me to exhibit patience even during our most difficult situations. When we do as we're commanded—when we "walk in the Spirit"— we will exhibit and live in patience (Galatians 5:16 and 22).

Reflecting the Heart of Jesus

From Genesis through Revelation, we see the patience of God repeatedly on display. In one instance, God the Father was patient with His sinful creation. He waited 120 years(!) before sending judgment through a worldwide flood, which destroyed all mankind from the face of the earth except for Noah and his family (Genesis 6:3).

Jesus, as God in flesh, also reflected this same heart of patience. He was patient with His disciples and their disbelief. He was patient with all those who were genuine in their desire to know and believe in Him. Can you imagine the patience the Creator of the universe possessed to work with a group of people—His creation, even His own family—who could not grasp what He was communicating about Himself? It is this same patience that Jesus extends to you. He knows you're a work in progress.

It is this same divine patience Jesus wants you to have and flesh out to others. So train yourself in patience. Lengthen your fuse. How long are you able to wait before you totally lose it? Try to extend your patience a little longer next time. And how many times can you withstand pressure before you crack? Try to make it a few more times when you're faced with future difficulties. That's where prayer comes to your rescue. Your patient God, the Lord Jesus, is willing to give you His patience. As He said, "Ask, and it will be given to you" (Matthew 7:7).

~ A Prayer to Pray ~

Lord Jesus, I thank You that You have been patient with me. I seem to take one step forward and two steps back. Help me live the patience You've shown toward me to others, whether with those at home, at church, or on the job. Give me a heart of patience that reflects Your heart. Amen.

Peaceful

*H*ow hard is it to find a place of peace these days? It certainly isn't Los Angeles, or at least it wasn't for me and my family. During our 35-plus years there, we experienced a home robbery, a hit-and-run to our car, a ring of fire on the mountains encircling our valley that required my husband Jim to stand on the roof, hose in hand, drenching our wooden shake roof to keep it from catching fire, not to mention two earthquakes that measured more than 6.0 on the Richter scale, one of which almost destroyed our house.

But never mind! It was home, and at the time I didn't notice what might be missing in my life. I'm not even sure if I could have properly described a place of peace. It wasn't until we moved to the Olympic Peninsula in the evergreen state of Washington that we finally experienced a true place of peace...five miles from nowhere!

And let me quickly add that a place of peace has also been hard for my two daughters to find. One was living in New York City on 9/11 when the twin towers of the World Trade Center were destroyed in a terrorist attack, and the other has been evacuated twice for hurricanes and once for a tsunami.

So, as we step out on another day's journey toward more Christlike character, we come to a most elusive quality and attitude, that of peace. Now, let me be quick to state that a *place* of peace is different than an *attitude* of peace, or peace in your heart and mind. If you want a place of peace, consider a move to some quiet place five miles from nowhere. But if you want to experience an attitude of peace wherever you are and no matter what's happening, move closer toward Jesus.

Before we look at the example of the One who is also known as the "Prince of Peace" (Isaiah 9:6), let's think through some truths about the attitude of peace:

- Our peace has nothing to do with our situation, and everything to do with knowing that we have a relationship with Jesus.

- Our peace has nothing to do with daily issues, crises, or the latest disaster, and everything to do with knowing that God is in control, that nothing is a mistake.

- Our peace has nothing to do with what we have or don't have, and everything to do with knowing that God will provide.

- Our peace is an inward attitude of tranquility and serenity that demonstrates a heart at rest, which we experience when, no matter what's going on around us, we put our complete trust in Jesus.

Jesus Shows Us the Way

Seven hundred years before Jesus was born, the Old Testament prophet Isaiah predicted the coming of the One who would bear the title of "Prince of Peace" (Isaiah 9:6). That person was Jesus. To start our look at peace as lived out in Jesus, let's fast-forward to the end of His life here on earth.

Jesus' Example of Peace

How Jesus responded to stress and turmoil is hugely helpful in growing toward Christlikeness. As Jesus neared death on a cross, He was in great conflict. So much so that He told several of His disciples, "My soul is exceedingly sorrowful, even to death" (Mark 14:34). In His humanness, Jesus, who was in all points tempted as we are, was having an issue—a temptation—with inner peace. He knew He had to suffer and die, but He still faced the stress of going through the actual reality of pain and death.

How did Jesus find peace as He headed toward a gruesome

death? He "fell on the ground, and prayed that if it were possible, the hour might pass from Him. And He said, 'Abba, Father, all things are possible for You. Take this cup away from Me.'" Then in full trust, Jesus said, "Nevertheless, not what I will, but what You will" (verses 35-36).

Nothing had changed. Jesus was still going to the cross. But now He was ready to do God's will. All had been settled and confirmed with the Father in prayer. As a result, with complete confidence and peace of mind, Jesus could say to His disciples, "Rise, let us be going. See, My betrayer is at hand" (verse 42).

Giving your fears over to a full trust in God is not the trust or belief found in salvation. It is the fruit of your salvation. It is the trust that comes when you face a painful or distressing situation and, instead of panicking or falling apart, you choose to believe that Jesus is there with you and for you, to uphold you and see you through.

Reflecting On Your Heart

Jesus offers you a choice. You can either choose to give in to feelings of panic or dread, or you can place your trust in Him and be filled with His peace. So, when the storm clouds loom and things seem to run out of control, trust in the all-powerful Son of God. When you do this, you will experience God's peace. Start with the little things (like "Lord, help me get through this speech," or "Lord, give me patience for one more hour until the kids are in bed," or "Lord, please get me through this family get-together"). Then when the really big dark clouds—your crosses to bear, your life-threatening trials—show up on the horizon, your trust will be strong and your peace will be to the glory of God.

Jesus Offers You His Peace

Jesus makes His perfect peace available to you in the following ways—and places:

THE PLACE OF PEACE

What's more comforting and peaceful than home sweet home? A place where you're surrounded by family and friends? Before His death, Jesus told His disciples He would soon leave them. They would continue on without Him, without His presence in the flesh. They needed to know that there would one day be a place for them, a place where they would be with Jesus Himself. To console them and calm their anxieties, Jesus told them, "Let not your heart be troubled; you believe in God, believe also in Me. In My Father's house are many mansions; if it were not so, I would have told you. I go to prepare a place for you. And if I go and prepare a place for you, I will come again and receive you to Myself; that where I am, there you may be also" (John 14:1-3).

THE PERSON OF PEACE

During Jesus' earthly ministry, whenever He sent the disciples out, if there were any problems or questions, they could always come back to Him. He was right there to help. Therefore, while Jesus was with the disciples, they were mostly able to hold themselves together. Now that Jesus was leaving, He wanted to assure them they wouldn't be abandoned. He was going to send someone who would serve as their Helper. How comforting that would be! They could have peace of mind knowing that Jesus would still be there with them through the Holy Spirit. He explained, "I will pray the Father, and He will give you another Helper, that He may abide with you forever" (verse 16).

The Holy Spirit is our personal Helper, Teacher, and Comforter (John 14:26). As you and I are obedient to receive instruction, guidance, and direction, the Spirit enables us to experience inner peace. When we abide in Christ and walk by His Spirit, we manifest the fruit of His presence—His peace (Galatians 5:22).

THE PROMISE OF PEACE

We've seen Jesus lovingly preparing His disciples for His death and departure. During Jesus' last months on earth, His disciples were His chief concern. Gone were the days of ministering to the crowds and the clamor of the multitudes. Jesus focused His attention on these fragile and confused men during His final days and hours.

As the end drew near, Jesus knew He must soon leave His beloved friends. It was time for Him to say His good-byes. Up to this point, without using the word *peace*, Jesus had promised His disciples a place of peace (heaven) and a Person of peace (the Spirit of Peace, the Holy Spirit).

Finally Jesus comforted them with these soothing, unforgettable words: "Peace I leave with you, My peace I give to you; not as the world gives do I give to you. Let not your heart be troubled, neither let it be afraid" (John 14:27). In New Testament times the customary way to say good-bye was to say, "Peace," or more specifically, the Hebrew term "Shalom." Even though Jesus was leaving His disciples, He was leaving them a legacy—"My peace I give to you." Once Jesus was no longer on the scene, His followers would have "peace with God" (Romans 5:1) because their sins were forgiven. And they would have "the peace of God" (Philippians 4:7) to guard their hearts and minds. The world cannot give this kind of peace, but Jesus can and does!

Reflecting On Your Heart

What is the one thing that will calm your fears and reduce your anxieties? Obviously it's not freedom from distractions or escapism. Amusements, hobbies, and travel aren't the answer either. The world offers such recreation as substitutes. In reality, only one thing— or Person—can offer you peace. And you know who that is. It's Jesus. And the peace He is offering you is different. As Jesus derived His peace from His relationship with the Father, so He is offering you His peace through a relationship with Him.

Is your life stressful? Do you need peace? Allow the Holy Spirit to fill you with Christ's peace. Give all your fears and anxieties over to Jesus in prayer. "Be anxious for nothing, but in everything by prayer and supplication, with thanksgiving, let your requests be made known to God; and the peace of God, which surpasses all understanding, will guard your hearts and minds through Christ Jesus" (Philippians 4:6-7).

Reflecting the Heart of Jesus

I'm sure you know by now that the attitude of peace is usually not your first response to most situations and possibilities. Maybe you get anxious over the physical safety of your family members, especially your children, as they are exposed to an evil world. Or you develop a knot in your stomach as you imagine a car wreck while you are moving down a highway at 70 miles an hour with four lanes of traffic whizzing by in both directions. You can have times of panic, terror, or dread in any number of situations. But remember, when Jesus offered peace to the disciples, He was also offering His peace to you. How can you experience that peace?

Pray. You can have the peace of Jesus by praying. Follow Jesus' example in the Garden of Gethsemane. When He was troubled, He prayed. Prayer is an act of faith. Prayer indicates you are coming to Jesus for His help. You are asking Him to provide whatever is needed to see you through your problem or situation, whether it's an issue at home or in your heart.

Obey. You'll experience peace when you follow the Holy Spirit's leading. Jesus was obedient to the Father's will and took the most difficult road—the road to the cross. His peace lay in His obedience to the Father. Your obedience will bring you this very same peace of mind and heart.

Trust. "Trust in the LORD with all your heart" (Proverbs 3:5). You will experience the peace of God...

...when you choose to trust in Jesus's presence and not panic.

...when you trust in Jesus' wisdom and ways and refuse to lean on your own understanding and wisdom.

...when you trust that Jesus knows best and you're willing to let Him lead in your life.

As you pray, obey, and trust in the Lord, you will reflect the peace only Jesus brings. Jesus walked this earth with perfect peace because He trusted the Father in and for all things. As you follow His example, you will reflect Jesus and be a living testimony of His saving grace and the peace of God that passes all understanding.

∽ A Prayer to Pray ∽

Dear Lord, thank You that Your mission was to bring peace to earth through Your death and resurrection. Help me to trust You with every area of my life so I can experience Your peace—a peace that goes beyond all comprehension, a peace that will guard my heart and mind against all fear and anxiety, no matter what. Amen.

Prayerful

*O*ften when I'm speaking at a women's conference, I describe the origins of one of my books. *A Woman After God's Own Heart®* had its beginnings through the gift of a little wordless book my daughter Katherine had given me on a past Mother's Day. After weeks of displaying the little book on the coffee table, during a dusting frenzy I placed it between two larger books in the bookcase. After all, I wondered, what could I do with a book filled with blank pages?

Several years later on my tenth spiritual anniversary, I sat in my living room thanking God for His saving grace. This time of prayer was followed by asking God what might be lacking in my life as a Christian. Before I could put the question mark on the question, I knew exactly what was missing—prayer! Immediately I jumped up and retrieved that wonderful little gift book from my then-12-year-old daughter and determined that I would start my new discipline of praying by using it as a prayer journal. Well, since then that small blank book has evolved into files—and even file drawers—of completed journals of asked-for and answered prayer requests. The book *A Woman After God's Own Heart®* came as a result of learning to pray about my priorities and roles as a Christian woman, wife, and mom.

Jesus Shows Us the Way

I think you would be in complete agreement with me when I

report that prayer is difficult. Yes, prayer is a blessing and a rich spiritual experience. But maybe it's because of our busyness, or lack of faith in the power of prayer, or whatever it might be, that we (or at least I) don't pray as often or as fervently as we should. Yet once again, as always and in all things, as we look at today's virtue, Jesus is the perfect model for prayerfulness. While we considered Jesus' faithfulness in an earlier chapter, we saw that He lived in a spirit of faithful prayer. He prayed alone with the Father in a secluded place, and He prayed in the midst of a crushing crowd. Prayer was His life, His habit. He prayed in every situation, in every emergency, at every opportunity, and for all issues. Nothing was too small to merit His prayers.

If you're dissatisfied with your prayer life (and who isn't?), then pausing to look at Jesus' habit of prayer can help provide you with marvelous inspiration and insights for developing a more faithful and consistent prayer life.

Pray for God's Will

Reading through the Gospels shows us many portraits of Jesus at prayer. You can't miss the fact that Jesus made it His habit to pray before important events and about important decisions in His life. For instance...

Jesus prayed as He began His ministry—Jesus' baptism was a significant milestone in His life. It heralded the beginning of His public ministry. How did He approach this momentous occasion? We find Him offering up His first recorded instance of prayer: "When all the people were baptized...Jesus also was baptized; and while He prayed, the heaven was opened. And the Holy Spirit descended" (Luke 3:21-22).

Whatever ministry you have pales in comparison to what Jesus did. Nevertheless, it is your ministry. And your ministry merits—and requires—your prayers, for it is the work that God has given you to do, according to His will, as it pleases Him, and for the benefit of His people (1 Corinthians 12:7,11,18).

Jesus prayed as He chose His disciples—Jesus had many followers, but He desired to choose 12 as leaders, as apostles, as "sent ones." These men would be given special authority to deliver His message to the world. Their selection would mark the beginning of the focused training of 12 men who would take the gospel to the ends of the earth. This was definitely a historic occasion. How would Jesus choose from all those who followed Him? Again, prayer was His answer: "He went out to the mountain to pray, and continued all night in prayer to God. And when it was day...He chose twelve whom He also named apostles" (Luke 6:12-13).

Reflecting On Your Heart

As a Christian woman, God desires that you disciple, mentor, and train "the young women" in your family, church, and Christian circles, faithfully teaching them "good things" (Titus 2:3-4). This calling from God is also a call to pray. So make it your goal to pray as you prepare yourself for this God-given assignment. Pray that you are friendly and available to younger women. Pray about how many gals you can spend time with. And, like Jesus, pray about which ones.

Jesus prayed before going to the cross—In this last scenario, Jesus' time on earth was coming to a close. His time of training His disciples was also over. In fact, He and the Twelve had enjoyed an event that is called the Last Supper. He knew His death on the cross was ahead of Him, and He knew its implications for all mankind. So He moved with His disciples to the Garden of Gethsemane, His customary place of prayer, to pray. His impending crucifixion would be excruciatingly painful and difficult, and His soul was in agony. Therefore He prayed.

The Lord's anguish had little to do with fear of the physical torture of the cross or even His death. No, He was sorrowful because the full cup of divine judgment against sin would soon be His to drink. How did Jesus handle this horrendous situation? "He...fell on His face, and prayed, saying, 'O My Father, if it is possible, let this cup pass from Me'" (Matthew 26:39). And, as He prayed a second and a third time, His prayers changed to reflect the powerful strength of His resolve: "O My Father, if this cup cannot pass away from Me unless I drink it, Your will be done" (verse 42).

You and I will never know or experience anything like Jesus did as He prepared for, faced, and endured death on a cross. But we do suffer—physical pain, emotional pain, lacks in our lives, difficult circumstances, challenging relationships, and more! To prepare for, face, and endure your suffering, you know what you need to do—pray!

Jesus shows you and all Christians the importance of praying when you need to make decisions and gain direction for your life. He prayed when He had to make an important decision or a special or trying occasion presented itself. His habit of prayer teaches us how to tap into God's power and grace, too. Jesus' desire was to follow the Father's will completely, and prayer was a vital part of His decision-making. The same is true for you as you seek to do God's will.

Reflecting On Your Heart

As you think about your life and the days ahead, what important event is about to occur? What guidance do you need for your future, or a child's future? What strength is lacking for an impossible but necessary decision? Follow the Lord's example and, like Him, pray. God has given you an effective resource in prayer. As one of my favorite prayer verses bids, "Let us...come boldly to the throne of grace, that we may obtain mercy and find grace to help in time of need" (Hebrews 4:16).

Pray for One Another

The book of Hebrews contains an amazing statement about Jesus' present ministry. Here we learn that "He is...able to save to the uttermost those who come to God through Him, since He always lives to make intercession for them" (Hebrews 7:25). Jesus' intercessory ministry started while He was on earth. Intercession for others—mediating for them to the Father—was a dominant feature in the prayers of Jesus during His time on earth...and still is!

For instance, on the night before His crucifixion, Jesus told His disciple Peter that the devil had asked permission to sift him like wheat, referring to an upcoming severe trial. Yet Jesus assured Peter that He—the Lord Himself!—had prayed that Peter's faith would not fail. Jesus had interceded and intervened on Peter's behalf (Luke 22:31-32).

Later on that same dreadful night, just hours before His death, Jesus poured out His great intercessory prayer in John 17. Notice the general content of His famous prayer for others, including you and me. First our Lord prayed for Himself, that He would glorify the Father (verses 1-5). Next Jesus interceded for His disciples (verses 6-19). He prayed that the Father would keep them from the evil one and sanctify them by the truth of God's Word. Then Jesus looked toward the future and prayed for all who would become believers, including you and me (verses 20-26). He asked for our unity, for the indwelling of the Spirit, and that one day all believers would be with Him in heaven.

Are you touched? To think that all those centuries ago, Jesus thought of us and prayed for us! Intercession for others was hugely important to Him. To focus on Himself was one thing, especially when He was looking at the cross. But to take the time, care, and love to bring His 12 disciples—and us—before God the Father, is quite another. Through Jesus' ministry of interceding for others, we can only conclude that if such intervention was important for Him, it is important for us as well to "pray for one another" (James 5:16).

These brief examples of Jesus' prayers for others (including you!) are a reminder that you're in a fierce spiritual battle. The Son of God's prayers should make you more aware that Satan and his forces are in a great struggle against God for the hearts and souls of men. For this reason Jesus interceded for His disciples, and continues to intercede for all Christians today—including you. He is praying that the Father would keep you set apart, holy, and pure, safe from the devil's power. Jesus also prays for unity in your church and among its members.

=== *Reflecting On Your Heart* ===

To reflect Jesus' heart for prayer, follow His example
and pray for others—for their protection from the evil

one. For their holiness. For unity among the people in your church and in the body of Christ. Knowing that Jesus is interceding for you should give you great confidence as you also pray, "Your will be done on earth as it is in heaven" (Matthew 6:10).

Pray to Your Father

When Jesus delivered His Sermon on the Mount, He described what's involved in kingdom living. He singled out a common practice among some of the people, especially the religious leaders, who wanted to be seen as "holy." These phonies used public prayer as a way of calling attention to themselves. Jesus called them "hypocrites" (Matthew 6:5), and cautioned His listeners and you and me, His readers, that our prayers are not for show. Jesus told His followers, "When you pray, go into your room, and when you have shut your door, pray to your Father who is in the secret place; and your Father who sees in secret will reward you openly" (verse 6).

Your prayers are for private communion with God. He and He alone is the audience of your prayers, whether private or public, and the One you should address. This doesn't mean it's inappropriate for you to pray in public. But it does mean that before you pray in public you should search your heart. Consider that God is the audience, your real audience, when you pray. It's not those who are hearing your prayers who matter, but God Himself.

Lord, Teach Us to Pray

Have you ever felt like you don't know how to pray at all? Maybe you've been to a Bible study or a class and during the prayer time everyone seemed to speak so naturally and at ease as they prayed and prayed and prayed. Afterward, when you walked away, maybe you were wishing someone could teach you how to pray.

It seems that Jesus' disciples had this same feeling. Many of them had watched John the Baptist pray. (Can you imagine?) Then, as they began to follow Jesus, they watched and listened to Him pray too. (And can you imagine seeing and hearing God in flesh at prayer?!) They witnessed His devotion to prayer and heard His passion. And they were getting the message—there is great power in prayer, and the benefits are many! So, after one of Jesus' times of talking with His heavenly Father, His disciples came to the Master of prayer and asked Him, "Lord, teach us to pray" (Luke 11:1).

Jesus' response? It was at this point that Jesus gave the disciples a model prayer, and that same prayer provides a model for you and every follower of Christ today. This prayer is found in Matthew 6:9-13 and is often referred to as the Lord's Prayer. But more accurately it's the Disciples' Prayer, for Jesus told them to pray "in this manner" (verse 9).

This model prayer is just that—a model. All those hundreds of years ago Jesus was giving a guide for all Christians for all time. He passed on a sample of some of the elements that we should include in our prayers. The best way for you to learn how to pray is to follow His model. Do what He said and pray as He prayed. The Lord prayed at all times for all things, and so should you. And He prayed faithfully and earnestly, and so should you. And He prayed for the good of God's people, and so should you.

Reflecting the Heart of Jesus

Prayer, for Jesus, was like breathing. It's as if He couldn't live without it. His one desire was to fulfill the Father's will. In His last recorded prayer to the Father before He was nailed to the cross, He said, "I have glorified You on the earth. I have finished the work which You have given Me to do" (John 17:4). How was He able to do this? Prayer was a major tool Jesus utilized for accomplishing the goal of fulfilling God's will.

The blessings of prayer await you, the blessings of communing with God. (Just think—you're talking to God!) The blessings of dealing with sin and growing more and more into the image of Jesus. The blessings of talking things over with God...before you make your decisions, and before you make too many mistakes. And the blessings of loving and caring for others enough to ask God to work in their lives. Best of all, building the habit of prayer into your daily routine builds Christlike character into your life... which leads to the blessing of reflecting the great heart of Jesus!

All of this—and more!—is accomplished through prayer. As the great Protestant reformer Martin Luther wrote, "The less I pray, the harder it gets; the more I pray, the better it goes." So, in the words of another saint, "The main lesson about prayer is just this: Do it! Do it! Do it! You want to be taught to pray? [The] answer is: pray."[11]

~ A Prayer to Pray ~

Jesus, I acknowledge the need, importance, and blessings of being a woman of prayer. Help me to "do it," to become a woman after Your heart who prays faithfully as You did. Amen.

Pure

I'm sorry, but I'm laughing as I think of the word *pure.* That's because just yesterday I had to move the half-gallon jug of maple syrup that's in my refrigerator to make way for something else. Seeing and touching that giant syrup container triggered my memory of purchasing it. I was in Maine visiting my daughter and her family, and we were out in her van on a day trip. For miles along the highway, we saw sign after sign after sign heralding "Maple Syrup Ahead." In my childhood home, my parents made their own maple syrup, always a favorite. So I could hardly wait to get some real maple syrup from a state covered with maple trees.

At last we made it to the roadside market, and I couldn't believe how many kinds of maple syrup there were! How would I ever decide which one to buy? Then I spotted the only brand that said on the label "100% Pure Maple Syrup." You guessed it—that's the one I purchased. (Too bad I didn't think about how I was going to get that giant jug of maple syrup on the plane and all the way back to Seattle, Washington!)

When you hear the words *pure* or *purity*, what comes to your mind? Unfortunately, it's not the quality of the foods we buy. In our society, most people think of sexual purity. But purity has broader meanings that apply to our minds and our spirits. Purity basically means that nothing is added to or taken away from a person or an object, such as gold or colors of paint.

Purity has become a strange and foreign concept in our society. Nothing is the real thing. Either something's been added or taken away from just about everything we know, use, and consume today. But there is one thing—or should I say one person—nothing has been added to or taken away from for all eternity. That person is God. He is the only eternally pure and unchanging being in the whole of the universe.

The Holiness and Purity of God

God is totally separate from all of His creation. He is unequaled. As Moses wrote, "Who is like You, O LORD, among the gods? Who is like You, glorious in holiness, fearful in praises, doing wonders?" (Exodus 15:11). Because God is holy He is absolutely pure and absolutely good. Therefore, He is untouched and unstained by the evil in the world. As such He can in no way participate in sin and evil. The prophet Habakkuk described God's purity, saying, "You are of purer eyes than to behold evil, and cannot look on wickedness" (Habakkuk 1:13).

God's perfection is the standard for our moral character and the motivation for our religious practices. God is flawless, and a similar standard is expected of those who would worship Him (Matthew 5:48).

Believers Are Called to Be Like God

Throughout the Bible it is repeated that believers are to be like God. As children of God we are to be like our Father, to reflect and represent Him. So, like Him, we are to be holy, which is to be pure. This is what the Lord God told the children of Israel: "Be holy; for I am holy" (Leviticus 11:44). We are to seek the same holiness that is basic to God's own nature. Now the big question is this: How? (or maybe, Wow! How?). Thankfully, Jesus shows us the way to attain this high and seemingly unattainable standard.

Jesus Shows Us the Way

There are only three pure humans who have ever lived—Adam and Eve (before the fall), and Jesus. And, because Adam and Eve did succumb to temptation and choose to sin, Jesus is the only standard by which we are to measure our human conduct, and that includes purity and holiness. Jesus tells us what is perfect and pure and He lives it for us! How should we respond to His purity and holiness? Observe the responses of the following people when they realized the purity and holiness of Jesus.

Depart from Me, for I Am a Sinful Man

Peter and some of the other disciples were followers of Jesus from the beginning of His ministry, but until Jesus formally called them to become disciples, they were still earning a living by fishing. It didn't take long for Jesus to attract a following—everywhere He went, a large crowd gathered. One morning Jesus approached Peter and his brother Andrew, and the brothers James and John, after they had fished all night and caught nothing. As the men were standing on the shore of the Sea of Galilee cleaning their nets, Jesus got into Peter's boat and asked Peter to take Him out just a little way from the shore. He wanted to get a better vantage point for teaching the large group of people who were pushing and crowding near the shore as they tried to hear Jesus (Luke 5:1-3).

When Jesus finished teaching, He asked Peter to steer the boat into deeper waters and throw out his fishing net. Remember, Peter and the others had fished all night with zero results. Peter, a professional fishermen, figured it would be pointless to try again. But because he respected Jesus as a teacher, he went along with Jesus' request. Miraculously, Peter and the other fishermen caught so many fish that their nets were breaking and their boats sinking. Suddenly Peter recognized Jesus as the Messiah and "fell down at Jesus' knees, saying, 'Depart from me, for I am a sinful man, O Lord!'" (verse 8). The prophet Isaiah had a similar reaction when he saw a vision of God. He cried out, "Woe is me, for I am undone! Because I am a man of unclean lips, and I dwell in the midst of a people of unclean lips; for my eyes have seen the King, the LORD of hosts" (Isaiah 6:5).

Peter saw no vision, but he recognized Jesus' true identity through the miracle that had just occurred and instantly became aware of Jesus' inherent holiness and purity. This revelation made Peter painfully aware of his own sinfulness and caused him to fall at Jesus' feet and confess his sin.

What are your thoughts about Jesus? Do you consider Him as simply a great teacher? A prophet? A good man? A powerful leader? Most people like reading "the stories of Jesus." But none of these views of Jesus will change your life radically from the inside out. Reasons like these will not move you to acknowledge your impurities, your sin. Open your eyes and heart. See Jesus for who He is. He is holy. Your purity begins when you recognize your sinfulness as well as Jesus' sinlessness and holiness, and you choose to seek for yourself the same purity that only Jesus can offer.

This Man Has Done Nothing Wrong

Peter recognized Jesus as God...and fell to his knees in worship and confession. Now note the variety of responses from three other people from a variety of walks of life.

Judas—When this disciple saw the awful injustice he had inflicted on Jesus by betraying Him for money, he tried to give back the 30 pieces of silver he was paid. As he explained to the chief priests and elders, "I have sinned by betraying innocent blood" (Matthew 27:4). Unfortunately, Judas never repented and ended up hanging himself. Judas' response was one of despair.

Pilate's wife—While Pilate, the Roman governor, was presiding over Jesus' trial, something rather amazing took place. Pilate's wife sent a message to him, saying, "Have nothing to do with that just Man, for I have suffered many things today in a dream because of Him" (Matthew 27:19). Pilate's wife saw Jesus as a "just" man, a man who was morally right and fair—and she wanted her husband to have nothing to do with condemning Him. Her response was to avoid Jesus.

The thief on the cross—Two thieves were crucified along with Jesus. One of them was convicted by all that took place. He saw how the religious leaders mocked Jesus and rejected Him. But the thief had a different response: He admitted he deserved to die because he had done wrong. He testified of Jesus' innocence, saying, "This Man has done nothing wrong" (Luke 23:41). "Then he said to Jesus, 'Lord, remember me when You come into Your kingdom.' And Jesus said to him, 'Assuredly, I say to you, today you will be with Me in Paradise'" (verses 42-43). The thief recognized Jesus' righteousness and holiness and responded in faith.

Truly This Was the Son of God!

If I were writing a biographical novel, I might describe the scene of the crucifixion something like this:

> The day started out with "business as usual" for the centurion and his men as they went to work. Unfortunately, their work included herding condemned prisoners to a place where they were to be executed by the most painful of all deaths—crucifixion. Their job was not to judge, only to carry out the judgment of others. On this day they escorted three men to be executed. But something unusual was about to happen on this particular day.
>
> One of the prisoners was different. His name was Jesus, and His only crime was that of being King of the Jews. After all the trials, examinations, and interrogations, this was Jesus' only crime. His purity as the perfect sacrifice was again affirmed.
>
> The soldiers watched as events began to unfold: Darkness fell, tombs were opened around them and the dead came out, and even in death this Jesus seemed to be different. These rough and brutal soldiers could only come to one conclusion: "When the centurion and those with him, who were guarding Jesus, saw the earthquake and the things that had happened, they feared greatly, saying, "'Truly this was the Son of God!'" (Matthew 27:54).
>
> While the religious leaders were celebrating Jesus' death, these heathen men recognized His innocence. They responded to the extraordinary things that were

happening. They observed Jesus' unusual responses
to His suffering and dying. As a result, they were the
first to proclaim Jesus as the Son of God after His
death.

The centurion and those with him responded in fear, and they
were right to be afraid. They had just witnessed something fearful
and terrifying. Unfortunately, the soldiers recognized Jesus as the
Son of God yet didn't respond in faith.

Reflecting On Your Heart

If you are a believer in Jesus, fear is not the response
He wants from you. Jesus desires your love, worship,
obedience, and purity. He has taken away your sin
and you are now free to live an abundant life. Thank
Him and praise Him with every breath. And don't forget this warning against disregarding purity: "If we
deliberately keep on sinning after we have received
the knowledge of the truth, no sacrifice for sins is left"
(Hebrews 10:26 NIV). Again, thank Jesus for His sacrifice. And purpose to live in purity.

Understanding More About Purity

Purity is high on God's list of priorities for women—It's very clear
in the Bible that God wants His women to be pure. In Titus 2:3-
5, God tells the older women in the church to teach the younger
women. Only six topics are listed for the older women to teach,
and purity is one of them: "encourage the young women to [be]...
pure" (NASB). This most definitely places our purity high on God's
list! Is purity on your "to do and to be" list?

Purity doesn't just happen—Because of our fallen human nature,
purity doesn't come naturally. In fact, the opposite is what comes

naturally! So you and I must make an effort to avoid people, places, and practices that could tempt us to impure thoughts and deeds. This means we must "flee…youthful lusts [and] pursue righteousness, faith, love, peace with those who call on the Lord out of a pure heart" (2 Timothy 2:22). Are you pursuing purity and cultivating a pure heart?

Purity comes from God's Word—The daily application of God's Word has a purifying effect on your heart and mind, "for the word of God is living and powerful, and sharper than any two-edged sword…and is a discerner of the thoughts and intents of the heart" (Hebrews 4:12). Are you hiding God's Word in your heart that you might be pure and not sin against Him (Psalm 119:11)?

Purity comes from confession—When you confess your sins, you are acknowledging your disobedience and thanking God that His Son, Jesus, has dealt with your sins on the cross. Confession is agreeing with God about your failure to live according to His standard of purity: "If we confess our sins, He is faithful and just to forgive us our sins and to cleanse us from all unrighteousness" (1 John 1:9).

Reflecting the Heart of Jesus

God's goal for you is purity and holiness. Therefore, your goal is purity and holiness. And your model is Jesus, who shows the way to purity and holiness. He is the only standard by which you are to measure your conduct. He is also the perfect model to imitate. Like all the areas of your life, God expects you to manage your purity. He has entrusted you with this most precious possession. Guard it well!

∽ Guard your physical purity. This will guide how you behave.

∽ Guard your mental purity. This will dictate what you think.

∽ Guard your spiritual purity. This will determine the depth of your devotion and worship.

~ A Prayer to Pray ~

Lord...

I give You all the desires of my heart—
may You bring them into line with
Your perfect will.

I give You my mind—
may it be filled with thoughts that could be brought
into Your holy presence.

I give You my mouth—
may I speak only that which honors You,
encourages others, and reveals a pure heart.

I give You my body—
may I keep my body pure so that it is
a holy and honorable vessel, fit for Your use.

I give You my friendships with men—
may I set my heart on purity.
May You have authority over all my passions.

I give myself afresh to You.
Take my life and let it be
ever, always, pure for Thee.[12]

Responsible

A s parents, Jim and I logged thousands (which felt like millions!) of hours training, hoping, and praying for our children to grow up responsible. We took parenting classes, read books, and met with other parents as we tried to learn how to instill this trait of all traits into our two girls. We even developed a system of assigning our girls a new responsibility, teaching them how to take care of it, and then rewarding them for showing responsibility in that area or for that task. We called it "learn one, earn one." Once they learned a responsibility, they earned a privilege or received a predetermined reward.

I'll never forget the day when our older daughter, Katherine, got her driver's license. She begged and pleaded with us for days. maybe even weeks, to let her drive herself and her sister Courtney to high school. No way did she want Jim or me taking her, and no way did she want to stay in a car pool. Finally Jim gave in, laid down the law, and gave explicit instructions on driving from home to school...and back. One reason we hesitated to let Katherine use the car was that it left me stranded at home. So once she agreed that she would run my errands on her way home from school, I got on board with the plan.

The Big Day finally arrived. I prayed with the girls, waved good-bye to them, walked back into the house, and fell on my knees and prayed until Katherine called me from school. She had made it! Hooray! At 3:00 in the afternoon I hit the floor again as she was to start on her way to the grocery store. She had my list, enough cash for the purchase, and I had guessed she and

Courtney would arrive home at about 3:45. Was I ever surprised when the front door opened at 3:15 and in they walked!

I did what every mom tries to remember to do—I asked if everything was okay, were there any problems, was one of them sick, etc. At last I said, "But weren't you supposed to pick up the groceries?" Well, I won't even try to describe my thoughts and feelings after Katherine said, "Oh, Mom, we were just too tired to get the groceries. All we wanted to do was get home."

You can well believe that we had a little discussion about responsibility after I blurted, "Well, welcome to the club! Every woman, wife, and mom goes to the grocery store tired!" And that's true—but we've learned to be responsible in that area. Others are depending on us, and we are faithful to come through and take care of that responsibility.

Now on to this stunning quality that so reflects Jesus. As you move through this chapter, keep in mind that, by definition, a responsible woman is one who's capable of being trusted to do something or finish something. She is competent and reliable. Others can depend on her to do what she says she'll do and to do it when she says she'll do it. If someone gives her a task, there are no worries about her or the task. She will complete it. She'll take care of it. Consider it done!

Jesus Shows Us the Way

We're on the move through our 30-day glimpse at Jesus and 30 character qualities He modeled among many more! If you want to be Christlike, then you'll need to be responsible. Jesus perfectly fits the definitions above...and more! He was totally reliable, totally dependable, and was completely trusted by the Father.

None of Them Is Lost

What's behind responsibility? One trait comes from the heart: A responsible person is concerned for others. Jesus was the most responsible person who ever walked the face of earth. Only Jesus, of all the people who have ever lived, perfectly fulfilled every task and every responsibility that was handed to Him. Whether it was fulfilling all righteousness (Matthew 3:15), making arrangement for the provision of His mother while hanging on the cross (John 19:26-27), or completing His mission of dying for sinners and being able to say, "It is finished!" (John 19:30), Jesus was responsible.

And here's another area of responsibility that Jesus was also able to complete: He kept His disciples safe. He acknowledged His successful completion of this charge to the Father as He prayed the night before His trial: "While I was with them in the world, I kept them in Your name. Those whom You gave Me I have kept and none of them is lost except the son of perdition, that the Scripture might be fulfilled" (John 17:12).

The disciples were kept under Jesus' protection and He lost none. You too can fully trust Him and depend on Him for your eternal life. He affirmed this on another occasion, saying, "I give them eternal life, and they shall never perish; neither shall anyone snatch them out of My hand" (John 10:28).

Reflecting On Your Heart

Jesus cannot lie. Therefore, when He promises protection, you can trust Him and take Him at His word. When you're facing temptation, or if you're looking at the reality of a life-threatening illness, you can know God's promise of eternal life is secure—not because it's a nice sentiment, but because of the power of Christ. Just as a shepherd protects his sheep, Jesus will protect you from eternal harm. You can trust the Good Shepherd to keep you, to provide for you, and to lead you home to heaven where there is "fullness of joy" and "pleasures forevermore" (Psalm 16:11).

He Appointed Twelve

A responsible person also makes plans for the future. Jesus always knew He was going to physically leave earth and return to heaven. As His time with mankind grew shorter, He had a plan for the future. He "called to Him those He Himself wanted. And they came to Him. Then He appointed twelve, that they might be with Him and that He might send them out to preach" (Mark 3:13-14). A responsible person knows that whatever is worth having is also worth saving and passing on to others. Jesus' plan was to pass on the truth of His message to a select group of men. Then, when He was gone, they would in turn pass it on to others.

Reflecting On Your Heart

What do you have that's worthy of being passed on to others?

~ As a Christian you are responsible for reflecting Jesus to a watching world.

~ As a Christian woman, you are responsible to teach and train another generation of godly women (Titus 2:3-5).

~ As a parent, you are responsible for teaching and modeling your Christian beliefs and standards to your children.

~ As a Christian wife, you are responsible to serve as your husband's helper and love him with Christ's love.

He Will Give You Another Helper

A responsible person leaves resources behind so others can fulfill their tasks. As you've read, Jesus knew from the beginning that He would one day leave this world. So He chose His men. Next, He began to train them for the months remaining before His death. Yet that brief training wasn't going to be enough. They would also need His strength and wisdom. As a responsible leader, Jesus knew the time limit on the in-person training He could give these future leaders. So He promised to send someone just like Him to continue the training, to empower them, to be with them, and more. As you read the promise Jesus made to His disciples, note how long the "Helper" would be with them: "I will pray the Father, and He will give you another Helper, that He may abide with you forever" (John 14:16).

The "Helper" Jesus spoke of was the Holy Spirit, who would advise, exhort, comfort, strengthen, intercede, and encourage the disciples, just like Jesus had until His departure back to heaven.

===== *Reflecting On Your Heart* =====

You probably know your personal physical limits. Yet you still have a vital part to play in the life of your family, your church, and community. And you probably have times when you find yourself stretched too thin by your numerous responsibilities. It's easy to become overwhelmed by the many hats you must wear. Unfortunately, you are limited to what you as one person can do. Yet, praise God, you have the Holy Spirit present and available to you when you "walk in the Spirit" (Galatians 5:16). So when you have more tasks than time or energy, look up. The Holy Spirit will give you "the fruit of the Spirit...love, joy, peace, patience, kindness, goodness, faithfulness, gentleness, self-control" (verses 22-23 NASB). These Christlike attitudes will help you get your work done God's way, in a way that reflects and honors Him.

Render to Caesar the Things That Are Caesar's

As we've seen many times throughout our journey with Jesus, the religious leaders of His day were continually looking for reasons and ways to discredit Jesus' life and ministry. Let's look at one of the occasions when Jesus was asked to answer an impossible question. It was basically this: Should the people pay taxes to a hated, oppressive, foreign government? What was Jesus answer? Once again the wisdom of God spoke as Jesus responded, "Render to Caesar the things that are Caesar's, and to God the things that are God's" (Mark 12:17).

Jesus was a responsible citizen. He never broke any civil or Old Testament laws. And He never taught His disciples to do otherwise. In this scene, Jesus was teaching responsibility to the government. The apostle Peter reiterated Jesus' teaching when he told believers to "submit yourselves to every ordinance of man for the Lord's sake, whether to the king as supreme, or to governors, as to those who are sent by him for the punishment of evildoers and for the praise of those who do good" (1 Peter 2:13-14). The context of Peter's teaching was how to live in the world in a way that brings glory to God, in a way that positively reflects and represents Him (verse 12).

Reflecting On Your Heart

No human government is perfect. Some people (even some Christians!) refuse to obey certain laws in their country because some specific legislation seems to be unfair or show favoritism. However, as a citizen of both the kingdom of God and your nation, you are responsible to both God and your government. Your reward is sweet indeed when you bear that responsibility well, for your good life filled with good works will bring honor to God.

Guidelines for Responsibility

God's will is not a secret. It's not hidden or cleverly imbedded in the text of the Bible. It's in plain sight, and the responsible Christian woman will make the effort to search out God's will for her life. When it comes to discovering and doing God's will, follow these guidelines for responsibility:

A responsible Christian is informed. Ignorance is no friend of the responsible Christian. In fact, it's a stumbling block to being reliable. Responsibility means doing the right thing, at the right time, in the right way. How can you know and follow God's will if you don't know His Word? Study God's Word to discover your responsibilities. Then live them. "Be diligent to present yourself approved to God, a worker who does not need to be ashamed, rightly dividing the word of truth" (2 Timothy 2:15).

A responsible Christian is obedient. A lack of knowledge or understanding is not an excuse for disobedience. God has already given you everything pertaining to life and godliness (2 Peter 1:3-4). How can you live in godliness and obey God's will if you don't know or don't bother to understand His Word? God is offering you an abundant, victorious life, but you must search for the wisdom of God "as silver, and search for her as for hidden treasures" (Proverbs 2:4). Then you will understand the will of the Lord.

A responsible Christian grows in faith. Like it or not, we are commanded to grow in the knowledge of Jesus (2 Peter 3:18). The New Testament is filled with commands, exhortations, admonitions, and encouragement to grow to spiritual maturity. The apostle Paul called it growing in "the fullness of Christ" (Ephesians 4:13). This maturity will give you a strong foundation and doctrinal stability. Then you'll know God's will and ways and won't be "tossed to and fro and carried about with every wind of doctrine" that comes along (verse 14). As in all things, the road to spiritual maturity passes right through the Bible.

A responsible Christian uses her spiritual gifts. The Spirit of Jesus has given spiritual enablements to you as a believer for the good of the other members of the body of Christ. "But to each one is given the manifestation of the Spirit for the common good" (1 Corinthians 12:7 NASB). You have been gifted and are therefore responsible to minister your gifts so others in the church are blessed. And your gift is needed and benefits others. Please be responsible! Discover your gifts. Develop your gifts. Minister your gifts "for the common good."

Reflecting the Heart of Jesus

Once again, look to Jesus. He fulfilled all His responsibilities to the very end, to the very last responsibility—going to the cross to pay the penalty for sin. This was indeed the ultimate act of responsibility for all time. Jesus sacrificed Himself as a ransom for your sins. The fulfillment of His responsibilities to the Father took Him to the cross. Where is fulfilling your responsibilities to the Father taking you? God is not asking you to die for Him. He's asking you to live for Him, to be a "living sacrifice" (Romans 12:1). Jesus possessed a heart of obedience that made Him responsible. If you truly desire to reflect the heart of Jesus, make it a priority to nurture a heart that is responsible to obey God and follow the example of His Son, the Lord Jesus.

～ A Prayer to Pray ～

Dear Lord Jesus, my heart's desire is to become more like You. As I learn about responsibility, I want my attitudes and actions to demonstrate that I am a living sacrifice, wholly acceptable to You. Thank You for the gift of Your Holy Spirit, who will help me to be responsible as a child of the King and a joint heir with You. Amen.

Sensitive

A s I sit here writing, Jim has just returned from getting our mail from our post office box. If we follow our usual routine, I'll pause in my writing and we'll sit down with a cup of coffee and start sifting through the pile looking for bills and important for-real mail. I don't know if it's because I just started writing this chapter about sensitivity or if this is the norm, but I'm always amazed by the number of appeals in our mail every day from relief groups, societies, missions, and individuals who are soliciting money.

Don't get me wrong. Jim and I have made it a goal to tune in to needs around the world and be generous and giving. Generosity is one of the character qualities Jesus possessed and we know God wants us to work on all the time. In fact, one reason we receive so much of this kind of mail is because we have given to so many worthy causes.

But I wonder—are Jim and I different in some way, or do you also get this same barrage of pleas for your money, time, and prayers? If you do, then you can probably relate to what I'm about to say: If you're not careful, you can begin to grow callous to these petitions, which are based on the actual needs of others. You know that you shouldn't have a hardened attitude, but when you're overwhelmed with a multitude of requests, sometimes it seems the only way to sort it out is to not sort it out! To just give up, withdraw, and become numb to the many needs around you.

This is when you and I need to take a fresh look at how Jesus handled a far greater onslaught of needs than we will ever encounter.

Jesus Shows Us the Way

As you begin a new day looking at this next marvelous quality in the life of Jesus, let's define what we're talking about when we speak of sensitivity. Sensitivity is being aware of your surroundings. It's sort of like having a "sixth sense" or "hurt-people radar." I'm not talking about wearing your feelings on your sleeve, or bursting into tears every time someone looks at you in the wrong way. No, I'm talking about noticing and picking up on suffering or anxiety in others. It's observing that something is lacking or not quite right, and realizing what needs to be done and moving into action to give the help needed. Jesus certainly showed us what it means to detect a need and do what's necessary to remedy that need. Let's learn from the Master as He walked among the people of His day. Some you'll recognize, and all benefitted from the Savior's "sixth sense."

He Healed the Sick

Jesus was supersensitive to those who were sick. In one instance He stopped into the home of His disciple Peter. Once there, Jesus was told that Peter's mother-in-law was sick. "So He came and took her by the hand and lifted her up, and immediately the fever left her" (Mark 1:31). In a compassionate response, Jesus, without a word, simply grasped her hand and raised her up. The fever left completely, and without any weakness, Peter's mother-in-law began to serve her guests.

A physical need is usually easy to detect. For instance, you have a friend or family member who's in the hospital. Or you hear of someone in your church who has cancer. You don't need to be a spiritual giant to determine these are opportunities to show love and give comfort. But what about the person whose illness is not so easily noticed or detected? This is where sensitivity is most needed.

===== *Reflecting On Your Heart* =====

How can you better discern what is needed by those who suffer silently and unnoticed? For one thing, pray. Ask God to open your eyes to those who are sick or heartsick, afflicted in body or soul. Pray for God to increase the range on your radar and your compassion level for others. And make it your aim to walk by the Spirit so you will respond and act with love, kindness, and goodness (Galatians 5:22-23).

He Had Compassion on the Hurting

Our Lord also noticed and tended to the bereaved. We see this occur one day in the town of Nain. There, Jesus came upon a funeral procession accompanying the coffin of a dead young man, the only son of his mother. The woman was now completely alone and without a close male relative, seemingly unprotected.

There's no indication that Jesus knew the mother or the son. Yet He stopped. And He stopped the procession. Why? Because His radar picked up on the woman's agony and distress...and He acted. "He had compassion on her and said to her, 'Do not weep.' Then He came and touched the open coffin, and those who carried him stood still. And He said, 'Young man, I say to you, arise'" (Luke 7:13-14). And the young man arose and was restored to his mother!

In His sensitivity, Jesus knew this widow's sorrow and her loss, and His heart went out to her in her hour of grief. When you are confronted with the suffering of others, how do you respond? You can turn away in indifference. Or you can reason "This isn't my problem. Surely there's someone who will or should help this person, whose role it is to assist her." Or you can emulate Jesus and reach out and do something yourself about a person's grief, suffering, and loss.

I often speak to women about "learning to look out," like a shepherd looks out for his sheep. I share some of the principles for ministering to others that I've learned to apply. The Bible says the eyes of the Lord "run to and fro throughout the whole earth" (2 Chronicles 16:9). So, when I go out in public, I intentionally look out for wounded sheep. And when I find one—and they are everywhere!—I make myself be direct. I send up a prayer to God and walk straight up to the wounded woman to see what she needs and what I can do to help.

Thankfully I've outgrown some shyness and hesitancy in this area of ministry. And I've overcome my natural tendency to hope someone else will come along, or to run and find a pastor or anyone more qualified than me to help with the person's problem. I believe that God has allowed *me* to find this particular person in need. What He asks of *me* is to be sensitive and aware, and to allow my heart to overflow with TLC—His tender loving care. I may need to involve others, but God allows me to be the point of first contact—the point of first love.

Reflecting On Your Heart

Jesus calls you to put up your people antennae, to cultivate His sensitivity to the needs of others, to ask, "How can I help?" and then to give "a cup of cold water" (Matthew 10:42) or whatever is needed.

He Will Not Cast Out Those Who Come to Him

With Jesus, there is no prejudice. He told the people, "All that the Father gives Me will come to Me, and the one who comes to Me I will by no means cast out" (John 6:37). And like Jesus, we are to respond without prejudice. Early in His ministry, Jesus decided to go back to Nazareth, the area around the Sea of Galilee where He grew up. While He was on the way, Jesus and His disciples stopped in Samaria at a popular well to rest, get water, and eat.

While the disciples were in town getting food, a Samaritan woman arrived at the well to draw water. According to the cultural traditions of that time, no respectable Jewish man would ever be seen talking to a loathed Samaritan, and certainly not to a woman. And never to a woman with a bad reputation like that of the woman at the well! But Jesus did. He showed no prejudice toward the Samaritan woman of ill repute. Instead, He asked her for a drink. By pursuing a conversation, Jesus caused a spiritual interest to rise up in the woman's heart. In answer to her questions, He said, "The hour is coming, and now is, when the true worshipers will worship the Father in spirit and truth" (John 4:23).

Are you watchful for opportunities to share the saving truth of the gospel of Jesus Christ? To speak so that a person might have her heart spiritually awakened? And to give others a chance to respond spiritually to the message of salvation through Christ? The gospel message is for every person, no matter what their race, social position, or religious background. You and I must be sensitive and on the lookout for situations that allow us a chance to share our faith in Christ with others. Jesus crossed all barriers to share the gospel, and we are privileged to follow His example.

He Cared for the Disabled

The Savior was also sensitive to the disabled. In fact, one Sabbath He stood and read a prophecy from Isaiah announcing that He would preach to the poor, heal the brokenhearted, recover sight to the blind, and set the oppressed free (Luke 4:16-21).

With His mission clearly in mind, on one occasion Jesus chose to enter Jerusalem through the Sheep Gate. Jesus had many options about which gate He used to enter Jerusalem. But because of His sensitivity to the disabled, He took this entrance, which caused Him to pass by a place where "a great multitude of sick people, blind, lame, paralyzed" were waiting for a miracle of healing to take place (John 5:3).

There, Jesus talked with a man who had been disabled for 38 years. He offered this poor man specific help, asking what seemed to be a strange question: "Do you want to be made well?" (verse 6). Jesus' desire was to make the man focus his attention and trust on Jesus—not on the water in the nearby pool, not on others who might help him into the water, not on a miracle of healing that many believed would occur to the person who entered the pool first after the water moved. Jesus was the only One who could help and heal this needy cripple, and he needed to look to Jesus alone.

Many Christians choose to avoid seeing and speaking to people with disabilities. It's easier to turn and go another way when someone comes toward you in a wheelchair. And it's easier not to look at or speak to a child on crutches who's struggling to walk. But, like Jesus, you and I can be sensitive and show compassion to those with disabilities. Unlike Jesus, we obviously can't help so much with their infirmities. But like Jesus, we can seek out these dear people, initiate conversations, and give specific help as we get to know them and learn more about their problems.

And most importantly, we can point them to Christ. That's what Jesus did. He chose to look for those in need, to be near them. He chose to talk with them. And He chose to direct their attention away from their physical issues and onto their spiritual issues. All this occurred because He was sensitive to those who were disabled.

He Loved the Unlovely

And what about the unloved...and the unlovely? As in all situations, Jesus shows us the way. Take, for instance, Jesus' encounter with Zacchaeus in Luke 19:1-10. To the Jews of Jesus' day, the most despised person in society was the local tax collector. We've encountered him before, and we meet him again now:

> Zacchaeus...was a chief tax collector, and he was rich. And he sought to see who Jesus was, but could not because of the crowd, for he was of short stature. So he ran ahead and climbed up into a sycamore tree to see Him, for He was going to pass that way. And when Jesus came to the place, He looked up and saw him, and said to him, "Zacchaeus, make haste and come down, for today I must stay at your house" (verses 2-5).

Here we witness Jesus again taking the initiative and reaching out to Zacchaeus. He noticed and looked at him, called him by name, and invited Himself to Zacchaeus's house. Afterward, as usual, the people complained, saying, "He has gone to be a guest with a man who is a sinner" (verse 7). Jesus' sensitivity to Zacchaeus's spiritual hunger was rewarded by Zacchaeus's response of faith: "Lord, I give half of my goods to the poor" (verse 8).

In every society certain people are viewed as outcasts. They are the unloved because of their occupation, political views, immoral behavior, or lifestyle. Don't give in to society's pressure, or even the pressures of certain "religious" communities. Jesus did not love sin, but He definitely did love sinners. His mission was "to seek and to save that which was lost" (verse 10). Praise God, Zacchaeus responded in faith to Christ's love.

He Was Spiritually Sensitive

To be like Jesus and reflect His sensitivity to any and all, pray for spiritual sensitivity. Look for those who are curious or seeking. Then take the initiative and extend Christ's love to the unloved and the lost. Build a bridge of love from your heart to theirs and help pave the way for Jesus to walk over that bridge right into their hearts.

The Savior was also sensitive *to those who desired to grow.* Not all of Jesus' seeking was directed to looking for and helping the sick, disabled, downcast, and despised. From the very beginning of His ministry, He sought and selected a few men who would carry on His work after His return to heaven. To do this they would have to be like Jesus and be sensitive enough to recognize those who sincerely wanted to grow spiritually. His selection process culminated after He prayed all night (Luke 6:12). Afterward, He chose 12 men "that they might be with Him and that He might send them out to preach, and to have power to heal sicknesses and to cast out demons" (Mark 3:14-15).

Sensitivity toward physical needs doesn't require much—except a heart that desires to help people and a willingness to reach out with help. We are also to be sensitive to the spiritual needs of others, committed to helping them grow and faithfully carry on Jesus' ministry.

If Jesus prayed, we must pray even more so—for spiritual sensitivity, for discernment about those who truly desire to grow in Christ. Another generation of women needs spiritual training and spiritual growth so they, in turn, can become godly women who will train and instruct the next generation (see Titus 2:3-5). Who can you teach? Follow Jesus' example. Pray for spiritual sensitivity as you look for and choose those whom you can mentor as the next generation of godly women. Take the first step: pray. Then start sharing what you know with your own children, nieces, and granddaughters.

Reflecting the Heart of Jesus

Over and over again Jesus took the initiative as He sensed the needs of others. Many people came to Him for assistance, and He was available and helpful to them. And just as often, He demonstrated great sensitivity as He went looking for those who needed His healing touch, His words of encouragement and instruction, or the assurance of His presence in their lives as they faced the future. Please don't hesitate to help others. And please don't wait on the sidelines when so many are needing your ministry. Do what Jesus did. Open your eyes—and your heart—and reach out!

～ A Prayer to Pray ～

Jesus, I know loving, serving, and helping others is all about my heart. Help me today to be more sensitive to those in need, to truly care about them, and act to better their lives. May my love shine brightly so others see You in my good deeds and glorify You. Amen.

A Servant

When you think of the "super servants" in your church, I'm sure at least one or two people pop into your mind. For me that special servant is Linda. From the moment Jim and I first attended our church, we've watched Linda reach out to those at church—including us—in a multitude of ways. Whatever anyone needs, Linda is like an angel that seems to flutter up at just the right time with precisely whatever is needed. In a selfish, self-serving world, she truly reflects Jesus as she willfully and joyfully serves the Lord and His people.

Serving is a unique quality that is a spiritual gift given to some members of the body of Christ (Romans 12:7). For these dear people, serving seems like their second nature. They love serving and somehow seem to know exactly what to do to help others. But even though helping appears to come naturally to them, it's really supernatural. It's God enabling them through the Holy Spirit to tend to the needs of others. It's a gift, a spiritual gift. But regardless of whether or not you have the gift of serving, you are commanded by the Lord to "serve one another" (Galatians 5:13).

Well, today is a red-letter day for us as we are blessed again to look at our dear, wonderful Jesus, the ultimate servant. Perhaps my favorite verse about our Lord is Matthew 20:28. I probably think about it every day: "The Son of Man did not come to be served, but to serve, and to give His life a ransom for many." One thing that touches my heart about this truth is that it is in the book of Matthew, the Gospel that shows us Jesus as the Christ, the Messiah, the King! And yet we read that serving was a strong quality in King Jesus' life—a priority and a way of life for Him.

Jesus Shows Us the Way

Isaiah is considered among the greatest of the Old Testament prophets because of his many predictions of the Messiah. For instance, you've probably heard this one during the Christmas season. It's Isaiah 9:6, and it's even been put to music in George Frideric Handel's "Messiah":

> For unto us a Child is born,
> unto us a Son is given;
> And the government will be upon His shoulder.
> And His name will be called
> Wonderful, Counselor, Mighty God,
> Everlasting Father, Prince of Peace.

What most people don't realize is that Isaiah also used the word *servant* many times to describe the nature of Jesus' earthly ministry. For example, He wrote, "Behold! My Servant whom I uphold, My Elect One in whom My soul delights!" and "Behold, My Servant... shall be exalted and extolled and be very high" (42:1; 52:13).

As you consider today's character quality of service, give praise to God that Jesus, the Messiah, the Savior of the World, came first as a lowly servant. Then open your heart and eyes and behold how the greatest man—and servant—who ever lived modeled what it means to serve.

Seek First the Kingdom of God

The Bible tells us that Jesus, very early in His ministry, was "tempted by the devil" (Matthew 4:1). Jesus in no way avoided this encounter. In fact, He was led by the Holy Spirit into the wilderness for a face-to-face confrontation with Satan (see Matthew 4:1-11). With each temptation, Jesus resisted Satan by quoting Scripture. Satan's last enticement was a trade-off of power and glory if Jesus would fall down and worship Satan. Jesus replied to the devil, "You shall worship the LORD your God, and Him only you shall serve" (verse 10).

For most women, the role of serving others is a given. If you're married, you have a husband to serve and care for. If you have children, well, add them to your "People I Need to Serve" list. And don't forget your parents and in-laws...and on and on your list goes!

So what is the biggest problem with serving? It's prioritizing. It's easy to get distracted in the course of helping others. If you're not careful, your service can become focused on people. Then one day you realize you've forgotten about your call to serve God. Jesus spoke to this priority when He said, "'You shall love the LORD your God with all your heart, with all your soul, and with all your mind.'" This is the first and great commandment" (22:37-38). Loving and serving God is the most important thing a Christian can do. It's to be your first priority. So "seek first the kingdom of God and His righteousness" (6:33).

I know your days are already packed with people and responsibilities, starting early with the blare of your alarm clock. Are you wondering, *Yes, but how?* The key is setting priorities—God's priorities. And He wants—and deserves—the Number One slot.

You Cannot Serve God and Mammon

Serving family is a good thing. But Jesus spoke of an area we are not to focus our service on—that of wealth and possessions. In Jesus' day the religious leaders loved money and what it could buy. One day as they were listening to Jesus tell a parable about being good stewards (Luke 16:1-12), Jesus pointedly ended with this truth: "No servant can serve two masters; for either he will hate the one and love the other, or else he will be loyal to the one and despise the other. You cannot serve God and mammon" (verse 13).

Obsession with money and possessions—mammon—can take God's rightful place in your life and take your eyes off Jesus. Wealth and goods can easily become your master. How can you tell if you're beginning to lose your focus on Jesus or starting to serve things and stuff instead of serving Jesus and His people? A few honest answers to a handful of questions will point to the obvious.

～ Do you often think on or worry about your money and possessions?

～ Do your finances or possessions often get in the way of serving God?

～ Do you spend a great deal of time taking care of your bank account, credit card accounts, investments, and possessions?

～ Do you have a hard time giving your money to further God's kingdom, support missionaries, or meet some need among God's people?

=== *Reflecting On Your Heart* ===

Those are some tough questions, aren't they? We are a blessed people. But that blessing can become a curse if money, possessions, a home, furniture, cars, etc., get in the way of serving God and His people. Examine your heart. If there's a problem with mammon, spend some time with Jesus and see how you can turn your priorities around. Remember, if you can't let go of your possessions, you don't own them, they own you!

The Son of Man Came to Serve

No one in the world, past or present, would ever suggest that Jesus was less than a great leader. What did He do that causes people to acknowledge "He was the greatest leader of all time"? Jesus never wrote a book. He never marshaled an army of soldiers. He never incited a political revolution. In fact, He never ventured more than a few days' journey by foot from His birthplace. So what was the defining mark of His leadership?

As Jesus' disciples observed the leaders around them, they seem to have concluded that greatness came from being a "lord" over others. So now there was a new lesson Jesus needed to teach the Twelve as His ministry on earth was nearing the end. They needed to get "greatness" in perspective:

Jesus called them to Himself and said, "You know
that the rulers of the Gentiles lord it over them, and
those who are great exercise authority over them. Yet
it shall not be so among you; but whoever desires to
become great among you, let him be your servant.
And whoever desires to be first among you, let him
be your slave—just as the Son of Man did not come
to be served, but to serve, and to give His life a ransom for many" (Matthew 20:25-28).

There may be a 2000-year gap between you and me and Jesus'
disciples, but they too had been affected by their culture. Their
world was filled with abusive force and dictatorial, authoritative
rulers. No one wanted to serve, so they would find someone else
to do the serving. For the disciples, serving and helping others was
the farthest thing from their minds. They wanted to be great! To
them, greatness was defined as lordship, not servanthood.

Like the disciples, you and I are products of our culture. As we
look around, we see that the majority of people are self-absorbed,
selfish, and busy thinking of ways to be served rather than serving. And like the disciples, we can have a hard time dealing with
the concept of serving. But our Lord Jesus came with a different
lifestyle and a radical life-message. He defined true greatness from
a new perspective. Instead of using people, we are to serve them.
Jesus' mission was to serve others and to give His very life away,
and you and I are to follow His example. We're to develop a servant's heart.

Reflecting On Your Heart

The best way to grow in this Jesus quality is to purpose that whenever you see a need, you won't wait
to be asked to help or wait for someone else to
do it. Open your eyes and ears. Who needs help?
Who's in your path? Then open your heart and hands.
Take the initiative and do what needs to be done.
Be Christlike—be a loving servant. This is what the
ideal woman in Proverbs 31 did: "She reaches out her
hands to the needy" (verse 20). And this is what the

widows in the church were assigned to do in 1 Timothy 5: They were to care for others, to lodge strangers,
wash the saints' feet, relieve the afflicted, and more.
They were to be "well reported for good works...dil-
igently [following] every good work" (verse 10).

You Are Worried and Troubled About Many Things

I can't tell you how many times I've taught and written about
those dear sisters, Mary and Martha. In fact, I've included them several times in this book. Poor Martha always comes off as the less-
spiritual sister. You know their story: Jesus was traveling and

> a certain woman named Martha welcomed Him into
> her house. And she had a sister called Mary, who also
> sat at Jesus' feet and heard His word. But Martha was
> distracted with much serving, and she approached
> Him and said, "Lord, do You not care that my sister
> has left me to serve alone? Therefore tell her to help
> me." And Jesus answered and said to her, "Martha,
> Martha, you are worried and troubled about many
> things. But one thing is needed, and Mary has chosen
> that good part, which will not be taken away from
> her" (Luke 10:38-42).

Jesus' message to Martha was on multiple levels. But please
don't miss His point about serving. As we've been learning, serving others is a good thing. And Martha was a true servant. She
loved Jesus and opened her home to Him. She delighted in cooking for Him and serving Him and the disciples.

But poor Martha also showed us that we can do our service
with a wrong attitude. Can't you just sense her attitude? She was
running around (literally spinning about) serving. Plus she was
upset that Mary had stopped helping her and was sitting—yes,
sitting by Jesus to hear His teaching. Well, Martha finally broke...
and broke into Jesus' time with accusations against both the Lord
and Mary.

You see, Martha was resentful of her sister. She gritted her teeth for as long as she could take it, then she came storming out of the kitchen, lashing out at Jesus, accusing Him of not caring and her sister of shirking her duties. Martha would have been better off not serving than serving with a bad attitude.

Reflecting On Your Heart

Do you ever find yourself with a "Martha attitude"? You're serving, but resenting every minute of it! You agreed to serve, but your heart just isn't in it. You would rather be the one being served! (Who wouldn't?) When this happens, remember Martha. Realize your problem and refuse to take your frustrations out on others. Instead, take a break. Step back. Go somewhere and admit your bad attitude. Ask Jesus to give you His servant heart for the work in front of you. Then, in the future, evaluate service opportunities before you say yes. Don't agree to serve if you're doing it for the wrong reasons—reasons such as peer pressure, expectations, pride, guilt, or a sense of duty. Your primary reason for serving is Jesus. He served you in the greatest way possible when He gave His life for you. And He wants you to follow His example, to be like Him. As He told His disciples, "I have given you an example, that you should do as I have done to you" (John 13:15). If Jesus, God in flesh, the King of kings and Lord of lords, the Messiah, the Christ, was willing to serve, shouldn't you be willing to serve?

Reflecting the Heart of Jesus

A woman who desires a more Christlike character realizes that cultivating a servant spirit is essential. Following in the steps of Jesus involves focused attention on developing the heart attitude of serving. And this noble quality begins at home with your family, right under your own roof. If you are married, God has given you the assignment of being your husband's "helper" (Genesis 2:18). That means your husband becomes God's priority person to receive your ministry of service. And if you have children, they're Number Two on your list of people to serve. Beyond this calling you are to serve all, to "serve one another" (Galatians 5:13).

Serving. It's a simple and noble assignment. And it is perhaps the most obvious sign of Christlike maturity. When you are serving others, your heartfelt, Spirit-filled service is a dazzling reflection of the heart of your Savior, the greatest servant who ever lived, the One who set the standard when He...

... served others whether it was convenient or not,

... served others whether they deserved it or not,

... served others whether they thanked Him or not,

... served others with sacrificial love, and

... served you by giving His life as a ransom for your soul.

～ A Prayer to Pray ～

O Lord, give me a heart of joy so I can follow in Your steps and gladly serve others. When my heart tires of serving, remind me of Yourself and Your holy hands washing the disciples' feet! May I become Your twin in selflessly tending to the needs of others. Amen, and thank You.

Submissive

*M*y husband Jim and I have been blessed with eight beautiful and healthy grandchildren. We are thankful beyond words to our Lord for this next generation. And we pray fervently that each boy and girl will grow up loving and serving Jesus.

Now, if you have children, you know all too well that parenting is not easy for lots of reasons. Even after all these years I can remember being thrilled that one of the first words out of the mouths of our own two sweet little girls was either "Mama" or "Dada." But it wasn't long before another word popped into their vocabulary. It was the word "No!" One of the major causes of conflict in parenting and in families is "the battle of the wills." Children resist following their parents' instructions because they want what they want without understanding the consequences or value of the things they desire. And unfortunately that battle of authority and submission continues as you and I, along with our children, struggle with submitting to people and God's will throughout our lives.

Jesus Shows Us the Way

As we continue to look at the qualities Jesus possessed, qualities we want to emulate as well, today's spotlight is on submission as seen in the life of our Lord. But are you thinking, *Wait a minute! Isn't Jesus God? He didn't have to take orders from anyone, right?* Wrong. Jesus' entire life on earth was spent in submission. That's why He is the perfect example for us to follow. So, if you have a problem with submission (and who doesn't?), with following others, then hopefully today's look at Jesus will instruct and motivate—and maybe even convict—you to make a few changes in your attitude.

But before we observe some instances of Jesus' submissiveness, let me explain a little about this concept. When I was writing my book *A Woman After God's Own Heart,* I did some research on this term for the chapter on marriage, entitled "A Heart That Follows." Here's a definition that struck my heart: "'Submission' (*hypotasso* in the Greek) is primarily a military term meaning to rank oneself under someone else. This heart attitude is lived out by leaving things to the judgment of another person and yielding or deferring to the opinion or authority of someone else."[13]

Before you start to chafe—or decide to skip this chapter, consider these instances of submission in our dear Jesus. Let's start with one of the earliest pictures of this quality in His life.

Children, Obey Your Parents

These words come from a verse in the Bible, Ephesians 6:1. Their purpose is to let children know their role in a Spirit-filled family. We see this scripture and the principle lived out in Jesus, the child. There's no biblical record of Jesus' life from His birth until He traveled with Joseph and Mary, His mother, to Jerusalem at the age of 12. Thinking the young Jesus was with some of the relatives who also made the journey, Mary and Joseph left Jerusalem for home, only to discover somewhere along the way that Jesus wasn't with the other travelers.

Joseph and Mary immediately rushed back to Jerusalem, where they found the boy Jesus in the temple "sitting in the midst of the teachers, both listening to them and asking them questions" (Luke 2:46). It's evident that Joseph and Mary didn't understand what Jesus was doing in the temple (verses 49-50). Even so, Jesus willingly exited the question-and-answer session and "went down with them and came to Nazareth, and was subject to them" (verse 51).

The relationship Jesus enjoyed with His heavenly Father did

not annul His duty to His earthly parents. He, like every one of God's people, was to submit to the fifth commandment, which states, "Honor your father and your mother" (Exodus 20:12). His submission to all the law of God—including honoring His parents—was essential to perfectly living out God's law so He could go to the cross as a righteous, sinless sacrifice for man's sin.

Honor Your Father and Your Mother

When you were a child at home, hopefully you were submissive and obedient to your parents. And if you're married, the new leader in your life is your husband. The Bible says you are to "leave" your parents and "cleave" to your husband, following him instead of them (Genesis 2:24 KJV). Nevertheless, married or single, you're to submit to God's Word and "honor your father and your mother" (Matthew 15:4) and their God-given role as parents for as long as they live.

Honor your parents. What does this mean? To honor means to speak well of your parents, to respect them, and to show all courtesy to them in their position as parents. The family is the foundational and fundamental relationship where submission is required. If you're a parent, the best way to teach submission to your children is by showing honor and respect for your own parents.

What is Jesus' message to you and me and every Christian? If the Son of God submitted to His earthly parents, and to the very end honored His mother even as He hung on the cross (John 19:26-27), you too should desire to honor your father and mother.

If You Love Me, Keep My Commandments

From the age of 12 until Jesus approached John the Baptist to be baptized and begin His earthly ministry, nothing is written about Jesus. That makes Jesus' encounter with John the first public event of His ministry. It marked His identification with those whose sins He would bear on the cross (Matthew 3:13-17). Jesus asked John to baptize Him. Knowing Jesus was the spotless Lamb of God (John 1:29), John initially resisted Jesus' request. But Jesus insisted, stating, "Permit it to be...for thus it is fitting for us to fulfill all righteousness" (Matthew 3:15).

Jesus was submitting to the Father's plan by preparing Himself to be the perfect sacrifice for sinners. In obedience to the Father, Jesus was identifying with sinners. The Father honored Jesus' obedience by speaking from heaven, "This is My beloved Son, in whom I am well pleased" (verse 17).

Reflecting On Your Heart

If you're feeling a little distant in your relationship with your Savior, perhaps it's because there's an area of submission that you're choosing to disregard. Take some time to search your heart. And be honest. This quality of submission is essential to pleasing Jesus and being like Jesus. It also demonstrates your love for Him, for, as He spoke, "If you love Me, keep My commandments" (John 14:15).

Live by Every Word from the Mouth of God

Immediately after His baptism, Jesus was led into the wilderness and spent the next 40 days without food. During that time, He was severely tempted by the devil. The Bible records three specific temptations (Matthew 4:1-11). How did Jesus deal with them? He defended Himself with Scripture, declaring, "It is written..." each time. In response to the first temptation, Jesus told the devil, "It is written, 'Man shall not live by bread alone, but by every word that proceeds from the mouth of God'" (verse 4).

Knowing, living, and submitting to God's Word is an effective weapon against temptation and the possibility of giving in to it and committing sin. The only offensive weapon provided in the Christian's armor is "the sword of the Spirit, which is the word of God" (Ephesians 6:17). Jesus used the sword of Scripture to counter the devil's attacks and shows us we should do the same.

Reflecting On Your Heart

To be truly effective, you are to submit to God's Word, not just quote it as if it is some form of magic. No, to be victorious and defend yourself against the "fiery darts of the wicked one" (Ephesians 6:16), you must submit to God through His Word, which will give you the power to "resist the devil and he will flee from you" (James 4:7). So read your Bible. Love God's Word and rely on it. Then when temptations come—and you know they will!—you'll be ready, with your "sword" always sharpened and ready.

Is It Lawful to Pay Taxes?

The religious leaders of Jesus' day had a problem submitting to Roman authority. In an attempt to get Jesus into trouble, they asked an impossible-to-answer question: "Is it lawful to pay taxes to Caesar, or not?" (Matthew 22:17). If Jesus said yes, they could accuse Him of being disloyal to the Jewish nation. If He said no, they could accuse Him of treason against the Romans. Jesus gave this now-famous reply: "Render...to Caesar the things that are Caesar's, and to God the things that are God's" (verse 21). Jesus acknowledged that we are to submit to governing authorities, and both Paul and Peter later repeated Jesus' teaching.[14]

When Jesus made His statement about submitting to the government, He did not qualify it by saying there were exceptions. He didn't say it depended on whether the governing authorities were good or bad. He only said that we should submit. The Roman government was brutal, condoned slavery, and held women and children in low regard. But not once did Jesus condemn the government.

We discussed the nature of the relationship between Christians and the government in our chapter on being responsible. But it needs to be repeated here so you and I don't forget how important it is to submit to an institution ordained by God. As with all forms of submission, we are commanded to subject ourselves to the laws of the land. God has placed governments over us to help protect us from evil.

Are there any exceptions to this submission? There is only one: We are to follow God's law and commands if we learn that obedience to the governing authority would require us to disobey God and His Word (Acts 4:19-20).

Take Up Your Cross and Follow Jesus

Jesus never sought great crowds to follow Him. His desire was to develop disciples. Therefore His message to follow Him pointed to the high cost of truly being His disciple. On one of the occasions when Jesus was surrounded by a large crowd, He stated, "Whoever does not bear his cross and come after Me cannot be My disciple" (Luke 14:27). And during a private gathering with His 12 disciples, He said, "If anyone desires to come after Me, let him deny himself, and take up his cross, and follow Me" (Matthew 16:24).

There's some history in Jesus' choice of imagery. The very mention of the word *cross* instilled fear in anyone living in a Roman territory. In that day, when a criminal was led to his execution he was forced to carry the instrument of his own death—a cross. This cross became a symbol of submission to Rome. Jesus chose this picture and process to get His disciples and the multitudes to think about their level of commitment to Him. To follow Jesus meant to live in total submission to Him—even if it might lead to death.

═══ *Reflecting On Your Heart* ═══

The cost of loyalty to Jesus hasn't changed. Following Him still comes with a price tag. Being a disciple wasn't easy in Jesus' day, and it's not easy now. A godless society still makes it difficult to be an authentic follower of Christ. Jesus isn't interested in a casual relationship with you, and He won't take a backseat to anything or anyone. You can prove that your commitment to your Lord is genuine—the real thing—by loving Him with all your heart and following Him with all your strength. You live for Jesus—and reflect and honor Him—when you submit to what He says and to His way of doing things.

Not as I Will, but as You Will

Wouldn't it be great to always know what God wants you to do and then do it? Our problem often comes when we think we have a better idea of how to run our lives. Eve had this problem in Genesis 3:1-7. Of course, she had a little help from the devil, who encouraged her to doubt God's ability to lead in her life. Unfortunately conditions haven't changed today. You and I, along with a little help from our sinful flesh and our pride, often willfully disobey God.

Sometimes we, like Eve, think we can live our lives just fine without God's help. But also like Eve, we soon find ourselves in terrible trouble. But Jesus didn't live like this when He was physically among His creation. He chose an opposite course of action as seen and heard in these scriptures:

> My food is to do the will of Him who sent Me, and to finish His work (John 4:34).

> I do not seek My own will but the will of the Father who sent Me (John 5:30).

> He...fell on His face, and prayed, saying, "O My Father, if it is possible, let this cup pass from Me; nevertheless, not as I will, but as You will" (Matthew 26:39).

Jesus was completely dependent of the Father for all His actions. As we've been learning, submission was His way of life. And as you know by now, it's to be our way of life too. And yet we sometimes think that God isn't really all that serious about us submitting to Him, His Word, and "to one another" (Ephesians 5:21), that surely this is an outdated concept. When we're thinking and reasoning in this way—or tempted to—we must remember that Jesus, God the Son, never thought it was beneath Him to submit His entire life to the Father's leading. Is there anything He's asking of you right now that you're balking at or refusing to do? Remember Jesus, who "suffered for us, leaving us an example, that you should follow His steps" (1 Peter 2:21).

Reflecting the Heart of Jesus

Jesus shows you a better way to live—the best way, His way—the path of submission. When you cease looking for ways to satisfy selfish desires and interests, you'll be free to willingly and whole-heartedly yield to Jesus and His ways. As you start submitting first and foremost to Jesus, you'll find it much easier to submit to others. It is then that you'll truly reflect the submissive heart of Jesus.

～ A Prayer to Pray ～

Dear Jesus, my life in You is a result of Your submission to the Father's will that You die for sinners—sinners like me. I thank You profusely with my heart and pray that my submission to You and Your ways will glorify You and reveal You to others. Amen.

Thankful

My husband Jim has been blessed with the privilege of traveling the world. These trips haven't been vacation travel for R & R. No, they were for visiting and assisting missionaries and teaching leadership conferences to pastors and church leaders in foreign countries. On one of his several visits to Russia, Jim was teaching at a Bible institute in Moscow. It was only September, but it was already snowing in that great city. The pastors in attendance had come from remote areas of this vast country. Most had traveled several days and nights to attend the week-long training conference.

Before Jim left the United States for the conference, he had been asked to pray about taking along any old suits to leave behind for pastors with clothing needs. Sure enough, Jim had several out-of-date suits that he packed for the trip. He didn't think much about it until the men on the receiving end teared up, gestured, and sought in any way they could to communicate their gratitude to him. They hugged him again and again. They prayed with and for him. They praised God for Jim and for the clothes. For them the used clothing was a great blessing from God.

I probably don't need to tell you that a different Jim landed on U.S. soil. He was absolutely overwhelmed by the gratitude these sweet men had shown. He was forever moved by the thankful emotion they had exhibited upon receiving the clothing he and the other lecturers had brought for them. To a man, Jim's ministry companions returned home with empty suitcases, regretting that they hadn't taken more clothing to leave behind. And the pastors in Russia? Well, they returned home wearing the only suit they had ever owned.

Jesus Shows Us the Way

Praise, thankfulness, and gratitude should be a regular part of our everyday life as Christians. Think about it—we have so much! But unfortunately our affluent society has dulled our sensitivity to God's grace and gracious provision. It seems to require a trip to a country where Christians are persecuted and deprived to wake us up to appreciate even the smallest blessings we enjoy as God's children.

As we continue walking through our gallery of qualities Jesus possessed, we come to the masterpiece of His thankful attitude. It is a truly amazing quality because, as the Son of God, He created and possessed everything. Yet He never failed to demonstrate a thankful spirit to His heavenly Father. As we spend time now looking at thankfulness, let's first thank the Father for "His indescribable gift" of His Son Jesus, our Savior (2 Corinthians 9:15).

He Must Increase

Jesus' cousin, John the Baptist, was very popular among the people of Israel. Large crowds followed him, heard him preach, and submitted to his call for repentance. At the peak of John's popularity, Jesus came to the Jordan River, where John was conducting his ministry. How did John respond to Jesus' visit, especially since many people were following Jesus too (John 3:22-26)? John responded with a generous, humble, godly attitude. He said, "I am not the Christ, but, I have been sent before Him…He must increase, but I must decrease" (John 3:28,30).

Expressing thankfulness and appreciation for others is often hard for people who are involved in the same line of work or, in the case of Christians, the same area of ministry. If we're not careful, you and I can become jealous of colaborers in Christ who are more gifted and can do a better job than us. We find ourselves feeling threatened by their abilities and by the attention they receive for their successes. But like John the Baptist, we must realize that these people are sent from God. And, also like John, we have a choice about whether we want to support or hinder their work. John realized that he was witnessing a superior being, one who was destined for great things. He thanked and praised God for Jesus, pointed others to Jesus, then stepped out of the way, knowing that he had fulfilled the role God had given him of announcing the coming of the Messiah.

Reflecting On Your Heart

Is there anyone in one of your ministries or at your workplace who has talents and abilities you don't possess? Don't feel threatened, and don't be jealous of their abilities. Jesus and John show you a better way. Step aside. See if there is anything you can do to assist that person. Speak well of her. And give thanks to God for the excellent way in which she does her work unto the Lord.

There Has Not Risen One Greater

John the Baptist had introduced Jesus to the people as the One who would bring judgment with His coming (Matthew 3:11-12). Later, when John was put in prison, he heard that Jesus was healing the sick, not bringing judgment as John had thought. Was Jesus the One? In his confusion, John sent several of his own disciples to ask Jesus if He was truly the Messiah. In response, Jesus sent John's disciples back to him as eyewitnesses of His many miracles.

Maybe John was a little discouraged. After all, he had been preaching for only a year before he was put in prison! As John's disciples left Jesus to tell John what they had seen, Jesus spoke to the crowd around Him. He praised John, telling them that John was "more than a prophet," and that "among those born of women there has not risen one greater than John the Baptist" (Matthew 11:9,11). Using Old Testament scriptures, Jesus shared God's description of John: "Behold, I send My messenger before Your face, who will prepare Your way before You" (verse 10). Hopefully

John's disciples returned to him with these words of praise, affirmation, and encouragement. Surely they reported what they had seen Jesus do and heard Him say in praise of John, their teacher.

John was indeed special! He was the one chosen to be the messenger, the herald of the coming Messiah. Jesus wanted the people to know how unique John was. He wanted them to know how thankful He was for John. And He wanted to ensure they didn't forget him. Being thankful for those who have helped you get to your present position is also an important part of an attitude of thankfulness. Jesus was grateful that the Father had sent John as His herald, His messenger. Unless someone preceded the King to tell people of His coming, how would they know that the King was coming?

Reflecting On Your Heart

It's easy to forget what others have done and sacrificed and contributed to help you get where you are today. Maybe it's your parents, or a former teacher, mentor, boss, or co-worker who showed you the ropes when you were new, or encouraged you when you weren't sure you could go on. Did you thank them when you were promoted? Do you continue to stay in touch and thank them for their support—past, present, and hopefully for their help and support in the future? The disciples had Jesus. Timothy and Titus had Paul. Mark had Peter. Mary had Elizabeth. Who do you have? Who is it you are grateful for? Express it to God, to them, and to others.

I Thank You, Father

After Jesus was rejected by the people in Nazareth (Matthew 4:12-13), He shifted His headquarters to the town of Capernaum, still in the area of Galilee. He performed many wondrous miracles in and around this area. Wouldn't you think the people would enthusiastically embrace Him as Messiah? Yet they showed complete indifference to Him. Jesus denounced their rejection and specifically singled out Capernaum (11:20-24). But then He did something a little unexpected. Rather than being downcast, He offered up thanks (or "praise" NIV) to His Father: "I thank You, Father, Lord of heaven and earth, that You have hidden these things from the wise and prudent and have revealed them to babes. Even so, Father, for so it seemed good in Your sight" (Matthew 11:25-26).

For what did Jesus thank or praise the Father? He thanked God for hiding the significance of His words and works from those who were supposedly the "wise" and "prudent." And He praised God that He had chosen to reveal Him and His message to "babes" instead, to those who were not formally educated, but humble and willing to receive the truth.

Reflecting On Your Heart

Has anything happened in your life that seemed odd or didn't make sense? Maybe you couldn't understand how a loving God could let something like that happen to you or a loved one. Well, you are not alone. Most people have events happen that are difficult or impossible to understand. Rather than question the Father, the Lord of heaven and earth, with your whys, take a page out of Jesus' life and be thankful. As the Bible says, "In everything give thanks; for this is the will of God in Christ Jesus for you" (1 Thessalonians 5:18).

Thank You that You Have Heard Me

Jesus had the 12 disciples, but He also had some special friends in Lazarus and his two sisters, Mary and Martha. Jesus had visited Bethany and their home many times because it was near Jerusalem. We've seen this trio before, but like the different colors in a rainbow, we can focus on and appreciate something different each time we view them. Here we see an encounter with them that moved Jesus to give verbal thanks to God.

As Jesus neared the end of His three years of ministry, He received news that Lazarus was sick. By the time Jesus and His disciples arrived on the scene, Lazarus had been in his grave four days. After meeting with the sisters, Jesus ordered Lazarus's tomb to be opened. Everyone was shocked as they thought about what they would see and smell! As they removed the stone from the tomb, Jesus offered up this prayer of thanksgiving: "Father, I thank You that You have heard Me. And I know that You always hear Me, but because of the people who are standing by I said this, that they may believe that You sent Me" (John 11:41-42).

Jesus and the Father had never been out of touch, so there was no need for Him to pray at all, or to pray out loud in public. But here, Jesus openly and publicly thanked His Father. Why? So all could hear! Jesus wanted those present at the graveside—and those of us today—to know and to give thanks that God is always there, and always listens when we pray.

Reflecting On Your Heart

You too can thank God that He hears your prayers. While you cannot presume to know how God will answer, you *can* know that God is good and that He cannot do anything that isn't consistent with His holy and righteous nature. Jesus said, "What man is there among you who, if his son asks for bread, will give him a stone?…how much more will your Father who is in heaven give good things to those who ask Him!" (Matthew 7:9-11). Thank God that however He answers your prayers, you can know it will ultimately be for your good and His glory.

Reflecting a Thankful Spirit

To the end of His earthly ministry, Jesus continued to offer up prayers of thanks and gratitude to the Father for all He had accomplished for and with Him, His Son. In His high priestly prayer in John 17, before His betrayal, Jesus…

... thanked the Father for the power and the opportunity to secure eternal life for all believers (John 17:2).

... thanked the Father for giving Him the disciples (verses 6-7).

... thanked the Father that believers had heard and obeyed the Father's Word, which Christ had spoken (verse 8).

Then, with a heart of thankfulness, Jesus turned His focus on the cross and His death. How could Jesus be thankful? And what was the reason for this grateful attitude? He knew the Father was in absolute control. He knew everything was going according to God's divine plan.

Is yours a heart filled with thanksgiving? Is there any reason you don't exhibit more of Jesus' thankful attitude? For instance...

> Maybe you don't know Jesus and are facing an unknown future without confidence. Ask God to grant you His grace to receive Jesus Christ as your Savior and give you the gift of eternal life. Then you too can be abundantly thankful (Ephesians 2:8-9).

> Maybe you are a Christian who's forgotten how hopeless your life was before you knew and belonged to Jesus. There is no greater gift than the gift of salvation. And, as with any gift, you should say, "Thank you"— constantly! Pause for a moment and thank God for His indescribable gift in Jesus Christ (2 Corinthians 9:15). Then purpose in your heart to respond with gratitude, praise, and joy to God for Jesus and the treasure of His salvation.

Reflecting the Heart of Jesus

Traditionally a Thanksgiving Day celebration is associated with giving thanks and expressing gratitude to God for the harvest of His bounty and provision. Praise and thanksgiving shouldn't be reserved and saved up only for a special, designated day. Exalting

God and giving thanks should be a regular part of every day. Thank Him before you get out of bed. Thank Him for each meal. Thank Him for family, friends, a good church, and His provision.

But thanks should not only flow from your lips for God and His gift of Jesus. You'll also want to lift up praise for people God places in your path. And you can express thanks to those people as well. You can never say thank-you enough to parents, friends, church leaders, and especially to immediate family. God has used each and every one of these people to mold and shape you into the woman you are today—a woman who reflects the heart of Jesus.

~ A Prayer to Pray ~

And now, O Lord, I bow before You with a heart of gratitude. In the words of King David, I marvel "Who am I, O Lord God" that You have blessed me so abundantly? For Your salvation, for the forgiveness of my sins, for my family and church, I offer You inadequate but sincere praise and thanksgiving. Thank You, dear Lord!

Truthful

grew up in a small-town culture where the telling of "little white lies" had developed into an art form. You see, it was unacceptable and even considered bad manners to hurt anyone's feelings. So, on occasion, one might need to stretch or bend the truth, or be purposefully vague, in order not to offend another person. For instance, if a person you didn't really want to spend time with asked if you two could get together, you would make up some story or reason why you couldn't.

Maybe you can imagine my difficulty when, at the age of 28, I became a Christian. Because I'd had some good teachers in truth-bending, I too had developed the fine art of the little white lie. Oh, they weren't big or terrible lies, just little ones—white ones! My culture had provided my models and examples for all those years, not to mention a very strong contribution made by my very own sin nature! As I looked at what God had to say about life in my brand new Bible, I began to discover the Jesus way of living. There I read, "Putting away lying, let each one of you speak truth with his neighbor" (Ephesians 4:25). And best of all, in Jesus I had a new model, a perfect example for living a life of truthfulness.

The Truth About Truth

Have you ever wondered where the concept and reality of truth and truthfulness came from? All things related to truth originated with God. For instance, consider these truths about the persons of the Trinity:

～ God cannot lie (Titus 1:2).

～ God is spirit and is worshiped in spirit and truth (John 4:24).

～ God's Word, the Bible, is truth (John 17:17).

～ The Holy Spirit, our Helper, is "the Spirit of truth" (John 14:17).

～ Jesus is the way, the truth, and the life (John 14:6).

～ Jesus is the living Word, full of grace and truth (John 1:14).

We'll look at Jesus' life of truth and His teachings in a minute, but for now, did you realize that telling the truth made it into the Ten Commandments? In Exodus 20:16, God said, "You shall not bear false witness against your neighbor." In other words, we're to tell the truth and nothing but the truth!

The Warning About Lies

Not only does God command us to tell the truth, He also hates lies and lying. David wrote of God in one of his psalms, "You shall destroy those who speak falsehood; the LORD abhors the... deceitful man" (Psalm 5:6). In Proverbs we read, "Lying lips are an abomination to the LORD" (12:22). And in another proverb God lists seven things He hates and considers to be an abomination to Him. One of them is "a lying tongue." And if that wasn't enough, another item on God's hate list is "a false witness who speaks lies" (Proverbs 6:17,19).

As women who love God and want to follow Him with all our heart and reflect the awe-inspiring qualities our Savior exuded, let's commit ourselves right now to seeking this virtue of being truthful...just like our Lord.

Jesus Shows Us the Way

Because Jesus was—and is—the truth, it's a little more difficult to pin down the evidence of this character quality in Him because He simply lived it. He was truth! But there are some statements He made that we can take to heart as we endeavor to speak and walk in truth.

I Tell You the Truth

Here's a study in opposites. In one of the many times Jesus argued truth with the Jewish scribes and Pharisees, He had this to say: "You are of your father the devil...[who] does not stand in the truth, because there is no truth in him...he is a liar and the father of it. But...I tell you the truth..." (John 8:44-45).

I hope you noticed the contrasts—the devil versus Christ; lying versus telling the truth. This is pretty clear, isn't it? And shocking! As one Bible commentator explains, "The attitudes and actions of the Jewish leaders clearly identified them as followers of Satan... They were Satan's tools in carrying out his plans; they spoke the very same language of lies."[15]

Reflecting On Your Heart

God and His Son, Jesus, make it painstakingly clear that lying has no place in a child of God. To follow God—who hates lying—means you are to tell the truth and refuse to lie. And to believe in Jesus—who is the truth and spoke the truth—means you are to speak only the truth. Do you wish to please God and to live—and speak—as His Son did? Then focus on living out the second half of Proverbs 12:22 and realizing its inspiring promise: "Lying lips are an abomination to the LORD, but those who deal truthfully are His delight."

Let Your Yes Be Yes, and Your No, No

Jesus was the Master Teacher. He was straightforward, simple, and clear with the truths He wanted His followers to apply. He spoke some very practical words in Matthew 5:37 that I find myself citing just about every day: "Let your 'Yes' be 'Yes,' and your 'No,' 'No.'" His message was, "Tell the truth! Say what you mean, and mean what you say. Do what you say you'll do or not do. Then others can trust you and believe you."

The practice in Jesus' day was—and this practice is still around today—to add an oath or to swear that what you said was the truth. But when your yes means yes and your no means no, there's no need to ever swear on anyone's grave or in someone's name. There's no need to expound on the fact that what you are saying is true or that you are speaking honestly. And there's no need to add any references to God being your witness. As Christians we are accountable to God for every word we speak. We should therefore speak only the truth and no more.

Paul Tells Us How

We've seen some bad news—God hates lying and liars. Well, thankfully, good news awaits us because the Bible is filled with help and instruction for becoming a woman who reflects Jesus and His truthfulness. The teachings and commands found on the pages of Scripture tell us how to deal with the age-old problem of choosing whether to tell the truth...or to lie. Look now at several truths that will help you walk and live in truthfulness. Treat these truths as a daily to-do list.

Putting Away Lying

First, Christians should be "putting away lying" (Ephesians 4:25). This means we're to have no part in lies and lying. We are to put lying away, set it aside, rid ourselves of it, and have nothing to do with it.

Instead, each believer is to "speak truth with his neighbor" (Ephesians 4:25). So out goes the old behavior—lying, and in comes the new—speaking the truth. The apostle Paul, the writer of these words, was focusing on unity in the church and the family of God. He knew that lying undermines trust and destroys relationships. I'm sure you know this to be true in your friendships, your marriage and family, among Christians, and even at work.

Speaking the Truth in Love

Paul wrote another bit of advice for us about truth. He said we are to be "speaking the truth in love" (Ephesians 4:15). Truth is truth, but without love, truth can come off as harsh, cold, or sterile.

In the words of British Christian leader and clergyman John Stott, "Truth becomes hard if not softened by love; love becomes soft if it is not strengthened by truth."[16]

How's your love quotient? Wherever you go and whenever you spend time with anyone—friends, neighbors, workmates, bosses, the people at church—you'll be talking for sure! And when your mouth is open, you need to make every effort to speak the truth, and nothing but the truth. And you'll want to consciously work at speaking the truth with love. It's a tall order, but it comes directly from God. So love it is!

If you have family at home, that's the best place to hone the habit of communicating truth with love. Every mom has plenty of opportunities to teach, train, and discipline her brood. How much better such instruction is received if it's delivered with a large dose of love. As a mom of two girls, I tried hard to implement the wisdom from Proverbs while getting vital information across to my girls' hearts. My favorites were—and still are:

‿ The heart of the righteous studies how to answer, but the mouth of the wicked pours forth evil (Proverbs 15:28).

‿ The heart of the wise teaches his mouth, and adds learning to his lips (Proverbs 16:23).

As you can see, you have to put effort into speaking the truth with love. When you teach your children in this way, guess what will happen? You'll also be teaching yourself to say hard and necessary truths in a loving manner. Once you learn the how-tos of truthfulness with family, then you're set to do the same with the many others who cross your path.

Be Not Slanderers

Because this book is about being a woman who reflects the heart of Jesus, I especially want to bring up gossip and slander. I've written in several of my books about my own difficulties with these two sins that come so easily, so naturally! The key verses—or, I should say, the key truths!—that penetrated my heart are passages that were written specifically to women.

The first scripture states that the wives of leaders in the church, or the women who serve in the church, "must...not [be] slanderers" (1 Timothy 3:11). The message is clear and obvious. The women who serve others in the church must not be gossips.

The other life-changing verse teaches that the older, more mature women in the church are to "not [be] slanderers" (Titus 2:3). Hmmm. Did you notice those words are exactly the same as in the previous verse? That means the message is the same. To serve or help other Christians, and especially the women in the church, requires that we do not slander or gossip about others. "Slanderer" is a word used 34 times in the New Testament to describe Satan. And, as we learned earlier in this chapter, he is a liar and the father of lies. He stands for everything that is the opposite of truth.

As I said, I had a problem—a b-i-g problem—with gossip and slander. But thankfully the truths in the Bible came to my rescue. And they will do the same for you as you pursue Christlikeness in your speech.

Reflecting the Heart of Jesus

Truth—and truthfulness—is a golden quality. And it's also time-less. It's changeless because it is connected with the changeless character of God. God cannot lie. He has communicated utterly unchangeable truth to you in His Word. And because He is truthful, you can believe what He says to be the truth. One of His promises was that He would send His Son, who also could not lie. Jesus was truthful at all times, even in the most difficult situations. He lived out truthfulness on a daily basis, moment by moment, and the Father was glorified by His consistent example.

As a woman who loves Jesus, I'm sure you desire to honor Him with your behavior, and with the words of your mouth. You reflect Him and act like Him when you allow the truth that dwells in you to control your speech and your actions. When you live and speak the truth, no matter what, you will reap a multitude of blessings. For instance...

~ Truth sets you free while lies enslave you to sin.

~ Truth binds hearts together while deceit destroys relationships.

~ Truthfulness is supernatural while lying is an easy natural response.

~ Truthfulness points you heavenward while lying lowers you to the deceiver's level.

~ Truthfulness is a grace that never goes out of style while lying leads only to disgrace.

~ A truthful woman will always be respected. And her honesty will always honor and glorify God.

~ A Prayer to Pray ~

Dear Lord of all grace and truth, thank You for speaking the truth so I can know You, believe in You, and trust You. You are the way, the truth, and the life. I pray that I will mature to the point that truthfulness becomes my way of life. Amen.

Virtuous

efore I even begin writing about a quality that sounds a little old-fashioned—that of being "virtuous"—I have to share with you that my first thought is of the Proverbs 31 woman. God's photo album of this remarkable woman appears in Proverbs 31:10-31. And the very first verse asks the question, "Who can find a virtuous woman? For her price is far above rubies" (verse 10 KJV). This virtuous lady's life is all about excellence. Because of her commitment to excellence she sought to do all things well, to live God's priorities, and to take good care of her responsibilities and the people in her life.

This woman is a godsend! She's there for me at all times. When I fail or flounder in my roles and responsibilities, I rush to these 22 practical verses for a refresher course on God's perspective on my life. When I sense my priorities shifting, this lady encourages me to keep on track. When I think I can't possibly go on or get it all done, a fresh look at her dedication and devotion restores my energy and renews my commitment to God's plan for me. When my vision is dimming, a visit with this woman who was praised by God rekindles my love for Him.

Discovering the Meaning of Virtuous

Virtuous. As I said, it sounds old-fashioned, even prudish. But what does it mean? As I did extensive research into the Proverbs 31 passage, I made my way through commentaries, doctoral theses, and numerous books that revealed the details of this woman's daily life. Here's something crucial I learned about the meaning of *virtuous* for the book I wrote about the Proverbs 31 woman, *Beautiful in God's Eyes*.

> The meaning of the word *virtuous* can be likened to the two sides of a coin. *Power of mind* (moral principles and attitudes) makes up the image on one side, and *power of body* (potency and effectiveness) makes up the other...The Hebrew word for *virtuous* is used 200-plus times in the Bible to describe an army. This Old Testament word refers to *a force* and is used to mean *able, capable, mighty, strong, valiant, powerful, efficient, wealthy,* and *worthy.* The word is also used in reference to a man of war, men of war, and men prepared for war...Just as mental toughness and physical energy are the primary traits of an army, they also mark God's beautiful woman.[17]

As we consider the character quality *virtue* or *virtuous* in the life of Jesus, I'll use synonyms such as *excellence, power,* and *goodness* along the way. Now prepare yourself for something wonderful! This is a truly magnificent life-changing quality!

Jesus Shows Us the Way

As in all things, Jesus shows us the way to virtue and excellence. Even though Jesus was God in human flesh, in His humanness He too faced discouraging situations and blocks to His progress. He got hungry, cold, thirsty, tired, and weary—just like we do. Yet He was faithful to pick Himself up and go on to do God's will. Look now at how He handled a number of situations with excellence. It was a virtue that prodded Him to keep on keeping on.

I Am Well Pleased

Jesus began His public ministry at about the age of 30 (Luke 3:23). What qualified Him to serve God? Answer: The virtuous way He lived His life up to that point. During Jesus' first 30 years, there are no recorded instances of miracles or visions or angels or the voice of God booming out of heaven. He simply lived a somewhat secluded life with His mother and siblings. He grew up, worked hard, cared for His family, got an education, and worshiped God along with others in His community. Like you and me, He was subject to the normal process of human growth and development, progressing intellectually, physically, and spiritually. The Bible explains that "Jesus increased in wisdom and stature, and in favor with God and men" (Luke 2:52). In other words, His progress received the approval of both man and God. Neither God nor men could fault His progress.

Does this normalcy sound a little mundane? Boring? Ho-hum? Unexciting? I mean, where are the fireworks? But realize these were not insignificant years. These were vital decades of preparation. Now for Jesus' report card: How well did He perform during those 30 years? Now God the Father's voice booms out of heaven! He powerfully spoke of His approval of Jesus as Jesus began His ministry and was baptized in the Jordan River by John the Baptist. God proclaimed for all to hear—and us to read today, "This is My beloved Son, in whom I am well pleased" (Matthew 3:17).

Looking back now and knowing of Jesus' approval, we can see that in all things Jesus had functioned in such a way—the way of excellence—that He received the Father's public approval. He had lived virtuously, according to the character and standard of God.

Reflecting On Your Heart

Obviously, God (and everyone you know!) knows that you aren't perfect. But He also knows you need a model, a guide to show you how to live and function in a way that would please Him. So God has given you His very own Son to show the way. If you want to know about virtue and see what excellence looks like, look at Jesus. And if you want to please God, look at Jesus. Do as Jesus did and take the time to grow and develop. Excellence is a process. It doesn't happen overnight. There is a course of action involved. So be encouraged—you are a work in progress. You can grow up in any areas where you are lagging behind. So work hard. Take care of your family. And be faithful to worship. And while you're growing, learn all you can about Jesus. Study His character. Note His virtue. Marvel at His excellence. Walk as He walked. Copy Him. Adopt His ways as your own. Reflect Him and His excellence, and you will mirror the character of God.

He Has Done All Things Well

Now fast-forward two years in Jesus' life, two years during which He was fully in the public eye. He and His disciples were constantly under the gaze of those who needed their help...and those who were looking for opportunities to discredit Jesus' life and ministry. During His travels, the crowds had become so intense that the Lord wanted to take His disciples to a more secluded area to get some breathing room. In fact, the Gospel of Mark tells us they "entered a house and wanted no one to know it" (Mark 7:24).

But there's no way the Messiah's presence could be hidden. So as people began to congregate, Jesus gave up His opportunity to rest and returned to His healing and teaching ministry, all evidence of His power and His goodness—in other words, His virtue. After these people watched and witnessed Jesus' ministry, how did they view Him? Their report was that "He has done all things well" (verse 37).

Jesus' days on earth were marked by excellence. It was a way of life for Him, and nothing deterred Him from it. Even under the suffocating presence of the crowds and the pressures of criticism, Jesus didn't let up. He refused to do anything halfway or half-hearted. He didn't try to get out of anything. And He didn't opt for shortcuts or try to sidestep responsibility. Because of His commitment to excellence, Jesus never gave less than His all to the people who surrounded Him.

Reflecting On Your Heart

Maybe you have some areas in which you excel... such as cooking or organizing or decorating or management. But the trait of excellence shouldn't be confined to a few limited spheres. As a Christian, excellence is to be your goal in every area and every role of your life. The "everys" even extend to include every task. Being virtuous is to be a way of life— your way of life! God's assignment is to nurture and develop excellence until it permeates every aspect of your thinking and actions, until it's embedded into your character. Whether it's as a wife, mom, or family member, or as a homemaker or employee, reflect Jesus' excellence. Do all things well.

You Shall Receive Power

Does the challenge of doing all things well overwhelm or discourage you? It sounds daunting, doesn't it? At times it may seem utterly impossible and could cause you to give up on growing in the glorious quality of virtue. But Jesus knew all about how difficult it is to do things well. And He's already provided exactly what you need. He's given you a "Helper," the Holy Spirit. Jesus first mentioned the promised Helper to His disciples after they were saddened when He told them He would soon leave. To encourage them, He said, "It is to your advantage that I go away; for if I do not go away, the Helper will not come to you; but if I depart I will send Him to you" (John 16:7).

Imagine their relief when the Twelve heard from the lips of the Lord that a "Helper" was on the way! The Holy Spirit would be there to guide, direct, and motivate them just as Jesus had when He was physically present on this earth. As a final assurance that He wasn't leaving the disciples without the resources they needed to serve Him, Jesus promised, "You shall receive power when the Holy Spirit has come upon you" (Acts 1:8).

Reflecting On Your Heart

What a relief! You have a helper! Like Jesus' early followers, you too can fulfill any service and undertaking and duty that falls on your shoulders, and do it with excellence! As a Christian, these goals are achievable because of the indwelling presence and power of the Holy Spirit. As you walk by the Spirit and are controlled by Him, you live out Christ's virtuous character. Equipped with this power, you can live excellently. You can have a positive impact on others. You can love Jesus and glorify Him by being responsible—virtuous and excellent—in all areas. As the apostle Paul exhorted, "Whatever you do in word or deed, do all in the name of the Lord Jesus" (Colossians 3:17).

Reflecting the Heart of Jesus

Think about Jesus and all that the quality of virtue enabled Him to accomplish. He had a to-do list from the Father. And He woke up every day to take care of that list. His checked-off chores looked like this:

- ✓ Keep the law
- ✓ Serve and minister to the people
- ✓ Go to the people and preach the gospel
- ✓ Go to Jerusalem…and go to the cross
- ✓ Fulfill all the Father's will

As a woman, you too have a to-do list from God, which includes taking care of yourself and your family, home, ministry, and work. As you pray over your list, remember Jesus. Let His faithfulness show you the way through your days. He didn't make excuses, let up, or quit. Instead He sought to accomplish the Father's will.

Like Jesus, your heart's desire is to please God. So take on Jesus' heart—a heart of virtue.

～ A Prayer to Pray ～

O wonderful Jesus! My heart is at a loss for words. A part of me faints at the thought of being virtuous and pursuing excellence in all things. But You have shown me the way. You have walked it before me. Help me to walk in it. Amen, and amen.

Wise.

*O*h *dear, another decision to make!* Has a thought like this ever rumbled around in your mind and heart? As one of God's women, I'm thinking your life is unbelievably complicated and demanding, right? You wear many hats, have a to-do list a mile long, and you're expected to live out your many roles and responsibilities—all while exhibiting a gentle and quiet spirit!

What's a woman to do? How can we always—or at least most of the time—make the right decisions, the ones that will honor Christ? As we near the end of our list of character qualities on dazzling display in Jesus' life, we are again blessed to look to Him as the One who had perfect wisdom and therefore provides the best model for us to follow in our quest for wisdom.

Jesus Shows Us the Way

The Source of All Wisdom

Jesus, as God, had perfect knowledge, and therefore acted in the light of all truth and facts. And, in His human perfectness, Jesus was also able to apply all truth and facts in untarnished wisdom. Wisdom displays itself in the choices made, actions taken, and words spoken. That's what true wisdom is—the correct application of knowledge. Today we want to look again at Jesus and especially at His wisdom. We need to understand how we too can develop the wisdom that will make us more Christlike not only in the way we live, but also in the decisions we make.

The Path to True Wisdom

Wisdom comes with the new birth that takes place at the moment of salvation, as the man Nicodemus found out during a secret visit to Jesus. We met Nicodemus in an earlier chapter in the context of courage. But today's highlight from his life centers on an encounter he had with Jesus early in the Lord's ministry. Nicodemus was becoming increasingly interested in knowing more about Jesus. One night this respected scholar and teacher came to meet and talk with Jesus. Though Nicodemus came at night in secret, he approached Jesus with an open and seeking heart, believing Jesus had answers. A teacher himself, Nicodemus came to Jesus with a teachable spirit.

Here's the scenario: A teacher in Israel is coming to the source of all wisdom to seek wisdom. What wise counsel did Jesus give to Nicodemus? He told him, "You must be born again" (John 3:7). In other words, if Nicodemus truly wanted the wisdom of God, he had to start all over. Once he was "born again" and became a believer in Jesus as Messiah, he would be empowered to live and act in a manner consistent with his new nature. He would experience the transforming power of salvation.

Reflecting On Your Heart

As you understand and accept the concept of being born again, wisdom becomes yours in Jesus Christ as He permeates your life. Here's how the path to true wisdom goes: First, with the new birth you receive eternal life, the power and guidance of the Holy Spirit, and wisdom. Then as you follow Jesus—the Lord, the Holy One, the light of truth—you become more aware of how Jesus wants you to act. Soon you start applying the wisdom you're learning to your decision-making process and begin making wiser decisions. Your speech too becomes more careful and gracious as you choose to speak wisely. Wisdom works its way from the inside out, beginning with your heart.

What Jesus told Nicodemus applies to you as well: You must be born again. If this is not true for you, you can start your life over today and begin walking in wisdom—His wisdom, heavenly wisdom. You can embrace Jesus and His saving grace at any time. You can be born again by receiving Him as your Savior.

The Quest for Wisdom

The Bible says that those who are in Christ have the mind of Christ (1 Corinthians 2:16). In Him we have the ability to grow in wisdom if we are willing to pay the price to obtain it. One of my favorite passages regarding wisdom is in Proverbs, a book of wisdom. As you read it now, you may want to grab a pen or pencil and circle the verbs that indicate what's involved in the quest for wisdom. Then we'll see what is involved in getting wisdom.

> My son, if you receive my words,
> and treasure my commands within you,
> so that you incline your ear to wisdom,
> and apply your heart to understanding;
> yes, if you cry out for discernment,
> and lift up your voice for understanding,
> if you seek her as silver,
> and search for her as for hidden treasures;
> then you will understand the fear of the LORD,
> and find the knowledge of God.
> For the LORD gives wisdom (Proverbs 2:1-6).

Search the Scriptures

The wisdom of Jesus we're considering comes from knowing His Word, the Bible. A psalmist in the Old Testament affirmed this when he cried, "Oh, how I love Your law! It is my meditation all the day. You, through Your commandments, make me wiser than my enemies" (Psalm 119:97-98).

The Jewish scholars of Jesus' day devoted their lives to studying the Scriptures—not to understand about Jesus as Messiah, but to possess superior knowledge and understand the "fine points" of the law (John 5:39). With knowledge as their goal, they missed the point of reading and studying the Bible. They missed the truth that Jesus was the Messiah. As Jesus said to them, "You search the Scriptures, for in them you think you have eternal life; and these are they which testify of Me" (John 5:39). Jesus was chastising these scholars because they failed to perceive the purpose of the Scriptures, which make known the Person and work and character of God's Son.

Christ is revealed in Scripture. And, as you and I read the Bible, we are changed into the image of Jesus. As the Scripture itself declares, "All Scripture is given by inspiration of God, and is profitable for doctrine, for reproof, for correction, for instruction in righteousness, that the man of God may be complete, thoroughly equipped for every good work" (2 Timothy 3:16-17). There is transforming power in the Word of God that empowers us and makes our behavior more Christlike.

Reflecting On Your Heart

Getting to know Jesus by reading the Bible will give you the knowledge you need to make wise decisions, better choices, and speak with wisdom. The Lord has a plan for your life—a grand plan. And as you search the Scriptures, you are perfected and prepared for that grand plan. You take on the heart of Jesus and the qualities He possessed as you are conformed to His image through His Word. And you do the works of Christ, who went about doing good (Acts 10:38). Simply said, the more you grow in your knowledge of Christ, the more He will be revealed to you and reflected by your life.

Ask of God

It's hard to fathom that Jesus, who was God in human flesh, sought the wisdom of the Father through prayer. From what we read in the Gospels and have noted several times in this book, Jesus was constantly talking with God the Father about decisions and issues He faced. He chose to restrict the use of His divine nature when it came to the decisions He made. He relied totally on the Father's wisdom for guidance. Even as He made His way to the cross He prayed, "Your will be done" (Matthew 26:42).

Prayer is the path to wisdom. All through your hectic day, ask God for help with any and every decision you must make. For some decisions, you can pray at length. And even in those times when you have only a split second to seek God's guidance, you can quickly ask, "Father, what is the right thing to do? What is the right thing to say?" In James 1:5 we read, "If any of you lacks wisdom, let him ask of God...and it will be given to him." Make this instruction—and the promise that accompanies it—your guide for making decisions and choices. So, in the words of Jesus...

> Ask, and it will be given to you; seek, and you will find; knock, and it will be opened to you. For everyone who asks receives, and he who seeks finds, and to him who knocks it will be opened (Matthew 7:7-8).

===== *Reflecting On Your Heart* =====

God's message to your heart is this: If you want wisdom, ask Him for it. But understand that when you ask for wisdom, you have to be ready to do what's required to gain it...and follow it. Be prepared to do whatever is necessary, like reading your Bible, obeying what you discover in God's Word, depending on God's leading through prayer, seeking the input of wise counselors, and following the examples of mature people who are already walking God's path of wisdom. Wisdom is calling out to you. Are you listening? Wisdom says, "I love those who love me, and those who seek me diligently will find me" (Proverbs 8:17).

Solomon asked for wisdom—One particular man in the Bible, Solomon, serves as an example of the wisdom in asking God for wisdom. You may already know his story. Solomon succeeded his father, David, as king of Israel. David was a great king who brought the 12 tribes of Israel under a unified kingdom. The tiny nation of Israel became a power to be reckoned with under David's reign. After David died, I'm sure Solomon was a little insecure with his new responsibilities as a king who was expected to follow in his father's powerful footsteps.

So what did Solomon do? First, the Bible reports that he loved the Lord (1 Kings 3:3). Therefore it was only natural for him to take the next step—he prayed. Solomon went before God and asked for wisdom. He essentially prayed, "Lord, please give me wisdom. Give me an understanding heart" (see verse 9). God honored Solomon's request and gave him wisdom, and Solomon became the wisest man in all Scripture until Jesus.

Rehoboam did not ask for wisdom—Now contrast Solomon with his son, Rehoboam (1 Kings 12:1-19). As the successor to his father, this young man was facing the same situation Solomon had faced: He was a new king and needed help with making decisions regarding the nation. Would he also seek wisdom from God as his father had? Sadly, he chose to follow the advice of his young and foolish peers. He made foolish decisions that ended up tearing the nation of Israel apart with civil war.

Reflecting On Your Heart

You don't have a kingdom to run, but you do have a household, your family, your finances, and your life to run. The results you reap will be affected by whether you choose to seek God's wisdom and direction, or not. Your decisions will have great consequences on you and on those around you. That's why it's wise to seek God's wisdom, to ask for His leading. Purpose to follow Solomon's example and ask God for wisdom on a regular basis.

Get Wisdom

Knowing we need wisdom is one thing. But we must also decide to do as Proverbs 4:7 tells us: "Wisdom is the principal thing; therefore get wisdom. And in all your getting, get understanding." Luke 2:52 says that Jesus grew in wisdom. And just as Jesus in His humanity went through all the normal growth processes, including growing in the wisdom that comes with experience and maturity, so we must see growing in wisdom as a process.

Wisdom doesn't come overnight, but you can accelerate your progress by making it a goal to get wisdom. How can you make this happen?

Step #1: Desire wisdom—"Happy is the [woman] who finds wisdom, and…gains understanding; for her proceeds are better than the profits of silver, and her gain than fine gold" (Proverbs 3:13-14).

Step #2: Pray for wisdom—"Yes, if you cry out for discernment, and lift up your voice for understanding…then you will understand the fear of the LORD, and find the knowledge of God" (Proverbs 2:3,5).

Step #3: Seek wisdom—"Seek [wisdom] as silver, and search for her as for hidden treasures" (Proverbs 2:4).

Step #4: Trust God's wisdom—"Trust in the LORD with all your heart, and lean not on your own understanding; in all your ways acknowledge Him, and He shall direct your paths" (Proverbs 3:5-6).

Reflecting the Heart of Jesus

Unlike Jesus, you will not always make perfect choices and decisions. But when you choose to submit to the Father's will and follow His lead, you will reflect the heart of Jesus. You'll find yourself viewing life from His perspective. You'll begin choosing better courses of action. You'll be blessed by the results of the wisdom you're applying, and so will the others in your life. You'll become the woman you want to be—a woman of wisdom. You'll become "the wise woman [who] builds her house...[and] opens her mouth with wisdom" (Proverbs 14:1; 31:26).

～ A Prayer to Pray ～

My Lord, You are "the wisdom of God" (1 Corinthians 1:24). You grew in wisdom, walked in wisdom, spoke wisdom, and lived wisely. You have set a pattern for me to follow. May the choices I make and the words I speak reflect Your wisdom. Amen.

Day 30

Worshipful

When my Jim teaches and preaches on worship, one of his favorite questions for the group is, "What is your most memorable worship experience?" This definitely generates some exciting sharing! Well, my most memorable worship experience occurred during an Easter service. I've always found Easter gatherings to be very moving, with special music and messages about Jesus' death, burial, and resurrection. I come out of those services inspired and longing to see Jesus like the women in the Bible did when they went to the empty tomb and were the first to see the glorified Lord after His resurrection.

Well, there I was, along with my husband Jim and a group from our church, sitting outdoors on a wooden bench under a vine-covered arbor, listening to a pastor give a message on Jesus' resurrection. What made this such an unforgettable event was the location where this service took place. We were at what is called "Gordon's Tomb" in Jerusalem.

Just picture in your mind what it was like to be in Jerusalem...on Resurrection Sunday...at this tomb...listening to a message on the resurrection...and singing the hymn "Christ Arose." And imagine that while all this is taking place, you are looking toward a tomb carved out of a rock wall with its stone door rolled to the side. Whether or not it was the actual tomb where Jesus was buried and rose again on the third day didn't matter. That time of worship was an amazing visual reminder that "He is risen!" (Mark 16:6).

Jesus Shows Us the Way

Before we step into the very personal quality of being worshipful, realize that worship, as an act, is defined as honoring or revering a divine being or supernatural power. It pictures great regard or extravagant respect, honor, or devotion.

We are so accustomed to focusing on worshiping Jesus and learning more about worship that we sometimes forget that Jesus Himself pursued serious worship. He attended worship in the synagogues in His hometown and in other towns across Israel. His prayer life—another avenue of worship—also shows a clear and passionate desire to commune with the Father. In fact, at times He prayed at great length, even all night. And He prayed with great intensity—we are allowed to witness in Scripture the difficult moments when He knelt in the Garden of Gethsemane and prayed in agony, so much so that "His sweat became like great drops of blood falling down to the ground" (Luke 22:44). And He prayed before making important decisions like choosing the 12 disciples (6:12-13).

It's very evident through Jesus' many overtures to the Father that Jesus was honoring the Father and seeking guidance and strength. So in a technical sense, Jesus was worshipful. But His worship went way beyond the technical aspect of prayer, way beyond His discipline and faithfulness to pray. He was actually in a constant state of worship because He was in constant communion with the Father.

As we end our 30-day journey toward becoming *A Woman Who Reflects the Heart of Jesus*, it is only fitting that we end with worship. And I want us to concentrate not so much on Jesus' activities of worship, but on our acts of worship toward Jesus. Hopefully and prayerfully, our survey of these select character qualities that defined Jesus has brought you to the point of wanting to stop and give praise to the Father for His gift of His Son. So, before we begin, take time to worship and give thanks to Him from your heart.

They Presented Gifts to Him

Worship is bringing the best we have to Jesus. That's what the wise men did. And their gifts weren't an afterthought. Their trip to find the baby born "King of the Jews" took possibly two years to make. When it came to gifts for the baby Jesus, they didn't just grab some souvenirs along the way or choose from among the things they had left over from their traveling. They chose to bring their best, their most expensive and desirable gifts. Then, "when they had come into the house, they saw the young Child with Mary His mother, and fell down and worshiped Him. And when they had opened their treasures, they presented gifts to Him: gold, frankincense, and myrrh" (Matthew 2:11). The wise men brought gifts and worshiped Jesus for who He was. This is the very core of true worship—honoring Jesus as God and giving Him what is valuable to us.

From the very beginning of biblical history, God has demanded that our offerings to Him be the best we have. Often in the Old Testament people faced judgment because they brought inferior offerings to God. Cain was judged because he brought an inferior gift to God. His brother Abel "brought of the firstborn of his flock and of their fat. And the LORD respected Abel and his offering, but He did not respect Cain and his offering" (Genesis 4:4-5).

You are to worship God because He is holy and your Creator. He is worthy of your worship and the very best you have to give. Because of Jesus' death as the Lamb of God who takes away the sin of the world, it is no longer necessary to bring animals to God to be sacrificed as part of your worship. What God desires from you is an offering of yourself. You are to present your body as "a living sacrifice, holy, acceptable to God, which is your reasonable service" (Romans 12:1).

Reflecting On Your Heart

As a woman who desires to reflect Jesus, you probably also desire to please God. That means not just going through the motions and disciplines of worship. It means involving your best in your worship—your best attitude, your best praise, your best obedience, your best-chosen heartfelt adoration, and your best self. God requires that you be your best—clean and holy—when you come to Him in worship. He asks that you

offer Him the gift of yourself as a living sacrifice. As
a yielded offering, you become an instrument of righteous service (Romans 12:2), and that pleases God!

She Gave Thanks to the Lord

Worship is also praising God for His gift of the Son. One of the
wonderful women in the Bible who understood the importance of
praise was Anna, a prophetess. This widow had devoted herself
to God since the death of her husband. She never remarried, but
instead, focused her attention on worshiping God. She "did not
depart from the temple, but served God with fastings and prayers
night and day" (Luke 2:37). And there she was, in the temple, the
day the baby Jesus was presented to the Lord. Anna was among
the first to see—and worship—the Savior!

Anna never left the temple, which means she made worship her
life's occupation. She may not have slept there, but for sure her
lifestyle was one of worship. And on one of Anna's worship-filled
days, Anna met the object of her worship. "At that very moment
she came up and began giving thanks to God" (verse 38 NASB).
Anna met the Christ child and praised God that this baby would
bring redemption for the nation (as promised in Isaiah 52:9).

Reflecting On Your Heart

Whereas Anna literally and physically worshiped God
night and day, you can do the same spiritually. You
can worship God anywhere and at any time through
prayer. You can give thanks to the Lord at all times
and in all places...and for all things. The more you
worship Him through prayer and praise, the more
you are aware of His presence. And the more you are
aware of His presence, the more you'll want to pray
and praise Him! As Jesus would later tell the Samaritan woman, you can worship God anywhere as you
worship in spirit and truth (John 4:23-24).

Worship in Spirit and Truth

As we've noted, worship does not require a place. The first time this truth was mentioned in the New Testament was from the lips of Jesus. You and I have visited this passage before, and let's see now what it tells us about worship.

While Jesus was on His way to Galilee, He and His disciples stopped at a well in what was known as Samaria. The disciples left Jesus to go into a village for food, while Jesus remained by the town's water source. When a certain woman—a Samaritan woman—came to draw water, Jesus entered into a discussion with her about worship. Both the Jews and Samaritans believed the location of a person's worship was what mattered most to God. Each group had their own place of worship, and each thought their place was the "right" place. They were like two rival sports teams!

It was to this woman that Jesus announced that "the hour is coming, and now is, when the true worshipers will worship the Father in spirit and truth; for the Father is seeking such to worship Him. God is Spirit, and those who worship Him must worship in spirit and truth" (John 4:23-24). With these words, Jesus made the place of worship secondary to our spiritual relationship with God. According to the Lord, our worship has two aspects:

- We are to worship in spirit—our human spirit. We are not to be thinking about a shopping list, or what's for lunch, or tomorrow's appointments. We are to focus our attention and praise toward God, making sure we are worshiping with the right attitude, that we are worshiping in heart and spirit.

- We are to worship in truth—consistent with God's revealed nature in Scripture. As we worship Jesus as God, the Word made flesh (John 1:14), He reveals the Father to us (14:6).

===== *Reflecting On Your Heart* =====

When you go to church, who are you worshiping and with what kind of attitude? Are you distracted from your focus on God? Are you thinking that as long as

you're there and everyone sees you, you have fulfilled your duty and done what's expected of you? If
this describes you, then you are not worshiping in
"spirit." And who are you worshiping? Is it the real
Jesus, God who took on human flesh and came to
earth to die a sinless death to pay for your sins? Or
are you worshiping a Jesus of your own making, one
you are not so obligated to obey? If this is you, then
you are not worshiping in "truth." Before you worship again, search your heart. Make sure you are worshiping both in spirit and in truth.

Hear Him!

Worship also demands your obedience. We don't think of Jesus
as ever taking a break, do we? He never seemed to need "down
time." But soon after He gave the first predictions of His death and
resurrection (Matthew 16:21), Jesus went into the mountains with
His three closest disciples, Peter, James, and John. While they were
there with Jesus, He allowed them a brief glimpse of His glory. The
disciples were awestruck and, as usual, Peter began talking. But he
was quickly interrupted by the voice of God. "While he was still
speaking, behold, a bright cloud overshadowed them; and suddenly
a voice came out of the cloud, saying, 'This is My beloved Son, in
whom I am well pleased. Hear Him!'" (Matthew 17:5).

Authentic worship from the heart results in submission and obedience to Jesus. The Father told the disciples to open their ears and
hear the Word of God in order to obey Jesus. And that applies to
all believers, including you and me. Jesus said, "If anyone loves Me,
he will keep My word; and My Father will love him" (John 14:23).

Reflecting the Heart of Jesus

Praise God! You are free to worship Jesus anywhere and at any
time. That means you can and should be in a continual state of
worship. You are always in God's spiritual temple. You can always

pray, praise, and pour out your heart in thanksgiving and petitions to an ever-present God. You can have an ongoing conversation with Him. The woman who abides in Christ, lives in His holy presence, walks by His Spirit, and worships Him with all her heart will truly reflect Jesus. So worship the Lord, all glorious above!

⌒ Praise to Offer ⌒

Jesus was born and lived in weakness, yet He was the recipient of all power. He was the poorest of the poor, yet He owns all the riches of heaven and earth. Jesus was mocked as a fool at His death, yet He is the wisdom of God. He was humiliated at His trials, yet He has received all honor and glory. He was made a curse on the cross, yet He has become a blessing to all who believe. The only fitting climax to this eternal plan of the Father is for all the universe to fall down and worship the only One who is worthy of worship and lift up praise to the Lamb of God as described by the apostle John in Revelation 5:11-14:

> Then I looked, and I heard the voice of many angels around the throne, the living creatures, and the elders; and the number of them was ten thousand times ten thousand, and thousands of thousands, saying with a loud voice: "Worthy is the Lamb who was slain to receive power and riches and wisdom, and strength and honor and glory and blessing!"

> And every creature which is in heaven and on the earth and under the earth and such as are in the sea, and all that are in them, I heard saying: "Blessing and honor and glory and power be to Him who sits on the throne, and to the Lamb, forever and ever!"

> Then the four living creatures said, "Amen!" And the twenty-four elders fell down and worshiped Him who lives forever and ever.

Notes

1. Gary Inrig, *A Call to Excellence* (Wheaton, IL: Victor Books, 1985), pp. 40-41. Quoting Bernard Ramm, *Them He Glorified* (Grand Rapids: Eerdmans, 1963), p. 89.

2. M.R. DeHaan and Henry G. Bosch, *Our Daily Bread* (Grand Rapids: Zondervan, 1982), June 14.

3. Curtis Vaughan, *The New Testament from 26 Translations,* The New English Bible (Grand Rapids: Zondervan, 1967), p. 22.

4. Genesis 39:4; Ruth 2:10; Esther 2:17; 5:2.

5. See Romans 5:2; Ephesians 2:8.

6. Charles R. Swindoll, *Esther: A Woman of Strength and Dignity* (Nashville: W Publishing Group, 1999), quoted in *Great Attitudes for Graduates!* (Nashville: J. Countryman, Thomas Nelson, 2006), p. 160.

7. *Life Application Bible* (Wheaton, IL: Tyndale House, 1988), p. 1825.

8. See Matthew 23:11; Luke 9:24; 13:30; 17:33; 18:14.

9. See Luke 10:38-39; John 12:1-2; 11:5.

10. See Mark 10:17-22; Matthew 19:20; Luke 18:18-19.

11. John Laidlaw (1832–1906), Scottish minister and theologian.

12. Elizabeth George, *A Young Woman After God's Own Heart* (Eugene, OR: Harvest House Publishers, 2003), p. 204.

13. George, *A Woman After God's Own Heart*, p. 77.

14. See Romans 13:1-7 and 1 Peter 2:12-14 respectively.

15. Bruce B. Barton, *Life Application Bible Commentary—John* (Wheaton, IL: Tyndale House, Inc., 1993), p. 185.

16. As cited by Bruce B. Barton, *Life Application Bible Commentary—Ephesians* (Wheaton, IL: Tyndale House, 1997), p. 86.

17. Elizabeth George, *Beautiful in God's Eyes* (Eugene, OR: Harvest House Publishers, 1998), pp. 13 and 15.

Personal Notes

Personal Notes

Personal Notes

Personal Notes

Personal Notes

Personal Notes

Personal Notes

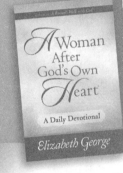

BIBLE STUDIES *for* BUSY WOMEN

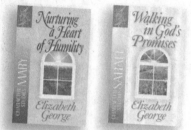

Books by Elizabeth George

- Beautiful in God's Eyes
- Breaking the Worry Habit...Forever
- Finding God's Path Through Your Trials
- Following God with All Your Heart
- Life Management for Busy Women
- Loving God with All Your Mind
- A Mom After God's Own Heart
- Quiet Confidence for a Woman's Heart
- The Remarkable Women of the Bible
- Small Changes for a Better Life
- Walking with the Women of the Bible
- A Wife After God's Own Heart
- Windows into the Word of God
- A Woman After God's Own Heart®
- A Woman After God's Own Heart®
  Deluxe Edition
- A Woman After God's Own Heart®—
  A Daily Devotional
- A Woman After God's Own Heart®
  Collection
- A Woman After God's Own Heart®
  DVD and Workbook
- A Woman's Call to Prayer
- A Woman's High Calling
- A Woman's Walk with God
- A Young Woman After God's
  Own Heart
- A Young Woman After God's
  Own Heart—A Devotional
- A Young Woman's Call to Prayer
- A Young Woman's Guide to Making
  Right Choices
- A Young Woman's Walk with God

Study Guides

- Beautiful in God's Eyes
  Growth & Study Guide
- Finding God's Path Through Your Trials
  Growth & Study Guide
- Following God with All Your Heart
  Growth & Study Guide
- Life Management for Busy Women
  Growth & Study Guide
- Loving God with All Your Mind
  Growth & Study Guide
- A Mom After God's Own Heart
  Growth & Study Guide
- The Remarkable Women of the Bible
  Growth & Study Guide
- Small Changes for a Better Life
  Growth & Study Guide
- A Wife After God's Own Heart
  Growth & Study Guide
- A Woman After God's Own Heart®
  Growth & Study Guide
- A Woman's Call to Prayer
  Growth & Study Guide
- A Woman's High Calling
  Growth & Study Guide
- A Woman's Walk with God
  Growth & Study Guide

Children's Books

- A Girl After God's Own Heart
- God's Wisdom for Little Girls
- A Little Girl After God's Own Heart

Books by Jim & Elizabeth George

- God Loves His Precious Children
- God's Wisdom for Little Boys
- A Little Boy After God's Own Heart

Books by Jim George

- The Bare Bones Bible® Handbook
- The Bare Bones Bible® Handbook
  for Teens
- The Bare Bones Bible® Bios
- The Bare Bones Bible® Facts
- A Husband After God's Own Heart
- A Man After God's Own Heart
- The Man Who Makes a Difference
- The Remarkable Prayers of the Bible
- A Young Man After God's Own Heart

Elizabeth George...

is a bestselling author and speaker whose passion is to teach the Bible in a way that changes women's lives. She has more than 5 million books in print, including *A Woman After God's Own Heart* and *Remarkable Women of the Bible*.

For information about Elizabeth's books or speaking ministry, to sign up for her mailings, or to purchase Elizabeth's books, please contact her at:

www.ElizabethGeorge.com

or

1-800-542-4611

or

Elizabeth George
P.O. Box 2879
Belfair, WA 98528